first 15

© First15

No part of this publication may be reproduced, distributed or transmitted in any form or by any means, including photocopying or electronic or mechanical method without prior written permission of the editor; except in the case of brief quotations embodied in critical reviews and certain other noncommercial uses permitted by copyright law. For permissions request, please write to us.

"Scripture quotations are from The ESV® Bible (The Holy Bible, English Standard Version®), copyright © 2001 by Crossway, a publishing ministry of Good News Publishers. Used by permission. All rights reserved."

Printed in Canada by Hemlock Printers

Contact: contact@first15.org
www.first15.org

Designed by Matt Ravenelle
mattravenelle.com

ABOUT FIRST15

Spending time alone with God every day can be a struggle. We're busier – and more stressed – than ever. But still, we know it's important to spend time alone with our Creator. We know we need to read his word, pray, and worship him.

First15 bridges the gap between desire and reality, helping you establish the rhythm of meaningful, daily experiences in God's presence. First15 answers the critical questions:

- Why should I spend time alone with God?
- How do I spend time alone with God?
- How do I get the most out of my time alone with God?
- How can I become more consistent with my time alone with God?

And by answering these questions through the format of daily devotionals, you'll practice the rhythm of meeting with God while experiencing the incredible gift of his loving presence given to those who make time to meet with him.

Allow God's passionate pursuit to draw you in across the next several days. And watch as every day is better than the last as your life is built on the solid foundation of God's love through the power of consistent, meaningful time alone with him.

To learn more about First15, visit our website first15.org. First15 is available across mobile app, email, podcast, and our website. Subscribe to our devotional today and experience God in a fresh way every day.

ABOUT THE AUTHOR

Craig Denison is the author of First15, a daily devotional guiding over a million believers into a fresh experience with God every day. In 2015, Craig founded First15 after sensing a longing in God's heart for his people to be about relationship – real, restored relationship with him – that above all else, he simply wanted the hearts of his people. Craig began praying, dreaming, and writing. And the idea of helping people spend the first fifteen minutes of their day focusing on nothing else but growing in their relationship with God was born. The vision was birthed in Craig's heart that if we as a people would worship, read, and pray at the beginning of every day, everything could change for the better. Craig writes, speaks, and he and his wife, Rachel lead worship to help believers establish a more tangible, meaningful connection with God.

———

CONTENTS

God is after the heart
Week 1

Honesty
Week 2

The posture of our hearts
Week 3

Sharing God's heart
Week 4

Day 1 - God's Relentless Pursuit	12-15
Day 2 - Made for Relationship	16-19
Day 3 - Identity of the Heart	20-23
Day 4 - An Open Heart	24-27
Day 5 - Be Who You Are	28-31
Day 6 - The Spirit and the Heart	32-35
Day 7 - Living from the Heart	36-39
Day 8 - Honesty is the Foundation	46-49
Day 9 - Facade	50-53
Day 10 - Tearing Down Walls	54-57
Day 11 - Fully Known	58-61
Day 12 - Fully Loved	62-65
Day 13 - Freedom in the Light	66-69
Day 14 - Living Honestly	70-73
Day 15 - Honesty before God	80-83
Day 16 - Honesty before Man	84-87
Day 17 - Acknowledging Our Need	88-91
Day 18 - Faith and Trust	92-95
Day 19 - Understanding	96-99
Day 20 - Surrender	100-103
Day 21 - Gaining Spiritual Eyes	104-107
Day 22 - God Wants to Use You	114-117
Day 23 - God is Already at Work	118-120
Day 24 - Declaring God's Glory	122-125
Day 25 - Light in the Darkness	126-129
Day 26 - Evangelism	130-133
Day 27 - Living Compassionately	134-137
Day 28 - Living Courageously	138-141

DAYS 1 - 7

God is after the heart

01

WEEK

"For the Lord sees not as man sees: man looks on the outward appearance, but the Lord looks on the heart." 1 Samuel 16:7

WEEKLY OVERVIEW

So often we view God as an enforcer of religious rules. We see the commands of Scripture as a list of to-dos rather than a path leading to abundant life. But those perceptions aren't the truth of Scripture. Those beliefs are founded on misguided notions of God's character. God is after the heart. More than he wants us to do right, he wants us to see him rightly. He wants going to church, reading the Bible, worshipping, serving the poor, and living righteously to come from a heart filled with a true revelation of his loving-kindness. May your heart be wholly God's this week.

God's Relentless Pursuit

DAY 1

DEVOTIONAL

The foundation for our faith is not meant to be built on our works or our understanding, but rather on God's relentless pursuit of us. We have relationship with our Creator not because we sought him out, but because he is always pursuing us. Any elements of Christian spirituality at work in our lives are the result of his

> *"Surely goodness and mercy shall follow me all the days of my life."*

PSALM 23:6

constant grace drawing us deeper and deeper into the abundant life Jesus died to give us. Faith built on anything else but God's pursuit is faith built on our own strength—an unsure and consistently failing foundation. Ephesians 1:16-18 says:

I do not cease to give thanks for you, remembering you in my prayers, that the God of our Lord Jesus Christ, the Father of glory, may give you the Spirit of wisdom and of revelation in the knowledge of him, having the eyes of your hearts enlightened, that you may know what is the hope to which he has called you, what are the riches of his glorious inheritance in the saints.

If we need a fresh understanding of God's pursuit we need only to pray as Paul did: asking God to enlighten the eyes of our hearts. We need only to look to the pages of Scripture and see story after story of God pursuing those who rebelled against him. The entire book of Hosea describes the heart of God to pursue Israel in a real-life metaphor of Hosea pursuing Gomer, who time and time again left him to prostitute herself.

There is nothing we could do to keep God from pursuing us. There is no sin too great, no distance we could run, that would discourage God from loving us. From the moment you were born God has been pursuing your heart. His greatest longing is for relationship with us. Don't let a wrong understanding of who God is cause your relationship with him to be works-based. Don't let your sin and failures get in the way of running to the open arms of your heavenly Father.

God is after your heart right now. He's sweetly knocking on the door of your heart that you might simply let him in. More than he wants you to do something for him today, he simply wants you to know he is with you and for you. Respond to God's pursuit today by giving him your heart. May your time of guided prayer be marked by a revelation of his loving-kindness toward you.

GUIDED PRAYER

1. Meditate on God's relentless pursuit of your heart. Allow Scripture to lay the foundation for a relationship built on grace.

"Your beauty and love chase after me every day of my life." Psalm 23:6 (The Message)

"We love because he first loved us." 1 John 4:19

2. Where has your relationship with the Father been founded on works rather than his pursuit? Where have you been trying to earn his affection? What parts of your heart have you withheld from him thinking he would reject you or chastise you?

"For by grace you have been saved through faith. And this is not your own doing; it is the gift of God, not a result of works, so that no one may boast." Ephesians 2:8-9

3. Give God your whole heart in response to his great love and grace for you. Open the door of your heart to him and rest in a revelation of his loving-kindness.

"Behold, I stand at the door and knock. If anyone hears my voice and opens the door, I will come in to him and eat with him, and he with me." Revelation 3:20

In Psalm 17:8 David prays, *"Keep me as the apple of your eye; hide me in the shadow of your wings."* May your pursuit of God be built on the truth that you are the apple of his eye. May your security be founded on the truth that he hides you in the shadow of his great wings. May your heart find peace, joy, and fulfillment today in the fact that God will never stop pursuing you.

Extended Reading: Psalm 23

Made for Relationship

DAY 2

DEVOTIONAL

We were made for relationship with our heavenly Father. We were made to know and be known by him. That one fact is meant to define both our identity and our actions. It's meant to lay the foundation on which we live, think, feel, and do. And it's only in living with relationship with God as our chief and central pursuit that our lives reflect his unceasing love and devotion.

"I will give them a heart to know that I am the Lord, and they shall be my people and I will be their God, for they shall return to me with their whole heart."

JEREMIAH 24:7

For a long time I've lived with wrong things at the center of my life. I've allowed earthly success, admiration of others, identity in my works, and an image of perfection to be the things that drove me moment by moment. And in those pursuits I only found disappointment, exhaustion, and unfulfilled longings. Even within the context of Christianity there is temptation to be led by that which is worldly, that which will never satisfy.

But in God there is another way. In the love of a grace-filled heavenly Father we can cease striving and start enjoying life founded on relationship with our Creator. Jeremiah 24:7 says, *"I will give them a heart to know that I am the Lord, and they shall be my people and I will be their God, for they shall return to me with their whole heart."* Within each of us is a longing to ground ourselves in our identity as the people of God. We are created to live out of the powerful knowledge that our God is real, knowable, loves us unconditionally, and has made his nearness wholly available to us.

You were made to live with the knowledge of God's love in every season. You were made to taste and see that your heavenly Father is good. You were made to live in constant communion with your Creator, that every moment would be filled with the abundance of his presence. God has life for you. He has love for you. And he won't rest until the entirety of your heart is his. God's love is entirely jealous while at the same time wholly sacrificial.

Give God your heart today. Center your life around relationship with him. Root and ground yourself in his unceasing love and faithfulness. May your life be forever changed as you set your eyes on the author and perfecter of your faith (Hebrews 12:2).

GUIDED PRAYER

1. Meditate on the truth that you were made for relationship with God. Allow Scripture to stir up a desire to center your life around God's unconditional love.

"I will give them a heart to know that I am the Lord, and they shall be my people and I will be their God, for they shall return to me with their whole heart." Jeremiah 24:7

"I have loved you with an everlasting love; therefore I have continued my faithfulness to you." Jeremiah 31:3

2. What are you valuing above relationship with your heavenly Father? What are you spending all your energy on? What's truly your greatest desire?

3. Tell God anything that you have valued above relationship with him. Know that his heart is not to condemn, but to set free and give abundant life. He longs to fill you with vision for the way in which you can most enjoy him and the life he's given you.

Oftentimes we look to the world to tell us what we should value over the Creator of the world. But in reality the world is a place filled with dissatisfaction and unrest. It's a place where even the rich, successful, and most loved must strive and work constantly to fulfill a longing only God can satisfy. Look to the Creator of heaven and earth for truth. Look to Scripture to decide what to pursue and value. And place your hope in God's promise of eternal, tangible satisfaction if you will center your life around relationship with him. May your heart find peace and rest in the always open arms of your loving Father.

Extended Reading: John 15

Identity of the Heart

DAY 3

DEVOTIONAL

Many of us spend our entire lives just trying to answer one simple question: "Who am I?" We look to our accolades and our strengths and weaknesses to define us. We look to other people to determine who it is we are. We allow circumstances and open or closed doors to tell us who we're supposed to be. We look everywhere but to the One who actually knows the true answer.

"I have called you by name, you are mine."

ISAIAH 43:1

But God says to you and me, *"Fear not, for I have redeemed you; I have called you by name, you are mine"* (Isaiah 43:1). 1 John 3:1 says, *"See what kind of love the Father has given to us, that we should be called children of God; and so we are."* And in Ephesians 2:19 Scripture says, *"So then you are no longer strangers and aliens, but you are fellow citizens with the saints and members of the household of God."*

We need a renewing of our identity. We need to look at the word of God and choose to believe that we truly are who he says we are entirely. We need to let our Creator define the identity of his creation. You serve a God who has called you his child. Regardless of anything you've done well or poorly, regardless of your successes or failures, you are first and foremost the redeemed child of the Most High God. It's time to anchor your identity to the unshakable truth of Scripture.

You see, it's not enough just to know what Scripture says. It's not enough to be able to recite verses like, *"we should be called the children of God; and so we are."* Until in your heart of hearts you believe the truth of Scripture, you will base your entire life on whatever it is you value most. If you value the opinion of man over God's word, your identity will be founded on the fleeting and fickle opinions of others. If you look to your circumstances to define you, then your identity will change with the passing of seasons. But if the identity you believe in your heart is founded on God's truth, then your self-worth, perspectives, decisions, insecurities, and beliefs will be unshakable and yield abundant life.

Take time today to assess your own heart. Look honestly at your beliefs. Where are you looking for your identity? Place your trust in the truth of God's word that the identity of your heart would come from your loving Creator. May your time in guided prayer be marked by a powerful revelation of truth.

GUIDED PRAYER

1. Meditate on the truth of your identity.

"Fear not, for I have redeemed you; I have called you by name, you are mine" Isaiah 43:1

"See what kind of love the Father has given to us, that we should be called children of God; and so we are." 1 John 3:1

2. What are you allowing to define you? What, in your heart of hearts, do you value above the truth of Scripture?

3. Ask the Holy Spirit for a heart-level revelation of who you are in Christ. Open your heart to God that he might reveal to you the truth of his perspective. Align your beliefs with the truth of Scripture.

It's absolutely critical to take an honest assessment of your heart when it comes to your identity. Don't let going to church, talking about Scripture, or even spending time reading God's word be enough. Take a look at what is actually sinking into your heart and changing your life. Don't rest until your life—your emotions, actions, and beliefs—align with God's truth. May you be energized and renewed to seek out the fullness of life God has in store for you.

Extended Reading: Psalm 139

An Open Heart

DAY 4

DEVOTIONAL

In order to experience all the fullness of life God has in store for us we must live with an open heart. Oftentimes, whether it be from wounds or simply bad teaching, we live closed off and self-focused. We go throughout our days with walls up around our hearts and rarely allow ourselves to receive the

"Keep your heart with all vigilance, for from it flow the springs of life."

PROVERBS 4:23

reality of God's nearness moment to moment. But God is calling us deeper. He's calling us to a lifestyle of encountering him. He's calling us to tear down the walls we've built up and trust that living openly and receptively will bear life, peace, and joy.

John 15:4 says, *"Abide in me, and I in you. As the branch cannot bear fruit by itself, unless it abides in the vine, neither can you, unless you abide in me."* God longs to be with you. He longs to speak to you, guide you, pour out his love on you, and remain with you throughout your day. He's not just a God of Sundays. His presence isn't only available at conferences, worship services, or monasteries. He is God of every moment. He is Lord of all eternity. And he longs to give you good gifts all the time. He longs to bear wonderful, life-giving fruit in you. But you must be willing to abide in him. You must receive all he has to give.

Proverbs 4:23 says, *"Keep your heart with all vigilance, for from it flow the springs of life."* Life comes from the heart both physically and spiritually. Just as the heart pumps blood out to the rest of your body, your heart pumps out spiritual life. Your heart is the place where God is constantly speaking. Your heart is what he cares about. It's not enough to just give him your mind for understanding or your hands for good works; he wants you at your core. He wants your life to be wrapped up in his.

Take time today to open your heart to your loving heavenly Father. Look for any walls you've built up around your heart. Stop believing any lies or misconceptions that would keep you from experiencing God's love moment to moment. May your time in guided prayer be filled with new life as your heart is open and receptive to the freedom of God's presence.

GUIDED PRAYER

1. Meditate on the importance of having an open and receptive heart to God.

"Abide in me, and I in you. As the branch cannot bear fruit by itself, unless it abides in the vine, neither can you, unless you abide in me." John 15:4

"Keep your heart with all vigilance, for from it flow the springs of life." Proverbs 4:23

2. Do you have any walls up between you and God? Are you living at times as if he isn't with you? Are you fully open and receptive to the things of God throughout your day?

3. Cast down any walls you've built up at the feet of Jesus and open your heart to him. Receive a revelation of his nearness and spend some time simply resting in his presence. Ask him to give you eyes to see all the good gifts he has given you today.

God is constantly blessing us. He constantly has good gifts to give us. James 1:17 says, *"Every good gift and every perfect gift is from above, coming down from the Father of lights with whom there is no variation or shadow due to change."* God longs to demonstrate his love to you by giving you good and perfect gifts. Cultivate a lifestyle of noticing and receiving God's blessings. Look for all the ways he is providing for you and give thanks to him. Live your whole life in light of the reality of his nearness and experience all his goodness throughout your day. May you be filled with abundant blessings as you seek to live with an open heart.

Extended Reading: Matthew 12

Be Who You Are

DAY 5

DEVOTIONAL

God will never ask you to be anyone other than who you are. He's not asking you to be just like other believers. He's not asking you to copy those around you that seem to be well-liked or accepted. So often we view God as a parent who spends all his efforts trying to fix us on the outside that we might keep up appearances. But it couldn't be more the opposite. God doesn't spend time trying to cover up who we are. Rather, he devotes himself to uncovering who we truly are—who he made us to be.

*"For you formed my inward parts; you
knitted me together in my mother's womb."*

PSALM 139:13

Psalm 139:13 says, *"For you formed my inward parts; you knitted me together in my mother's womb."* God formed you wonderfully and uniquely. He gave you a personality and calling all your own. He sees past all the exteriors we create to try and fit in. He sees through all our efforts to cover up what makes us unique and different. He sees us for who we really are. And he is calling us to cast down our facades and live out of the revelation that we are already, right now, fully loved and accepted by our Creator.

Discovering your identity begins with a journey with God to your heart. If you're wondering who you truly are, you need not look past yourself, but rather, with the Holy Spirit, take an honest look at yourself. Don't shy away from your insecurities. Don't shy away from that which makes you different. Allow God to reveal how he sees you. Allow him to reveal to you the true desires of your heart. And allow him to lay a secure foundation for you built on his unconditional love that you might live vulnerably and honestly.

Allow God to fill you with the courage to be yourself today. Stop trying to change yourself to fit in to the expectations of others. And live with your identity and value securely founded in the love of your heavenly Father.

Spend some time in guided prayer looking at your heart with the Holy Spirit. Allow him to reveal how he sees you. Ask him how he has formed you and made you unique. And allow him to empower you to be yourself today. May your time in guided prayer be filled with freedom and courage as you cease striving to be someone that you're not.

GUIDED PRAYER

1. Meditate on God's call for you to be who you are. Allow Scripture to fill you with a desire to live honestly.

"For you formed my inward parts; you knitted me together in my mother's womb." Psalm 139:13

"As in water face reflects face, so the heart of man reflects the man." Proverbs 27:19

2. In what ways are you striving to be someone you're not? How are you seeking to keep up appearances rather than live honestly?

3. Ask the Holy Spirit to reveal how he sees you. Ask him to fill you with courage to cast down any facades and be who you truly are.

Matthew 6:21 says, *"For where your treasure is, there your heart will be also."* If you choose to place value and identity on what God says about you, then your heart will find freedom that transcends the ways and cares of the world. Treasure what God says about you. Store up his words and truth over you. Let them be your source of hope and life. May your heart be with your loving, kind heavenly Father as you seek to find freedom to live as you truly are today.

Extended Reading: Matthew 6

The Spirit and the Heart

DAY 6

DEVOTIONAL

Abundant life is given in the communion of the Spirit and the heart. It's our hearts the Spirit speaks to. It's our hearts he fills with love, joy, peace, and hope. It's our hearts in which he dwells. To acknowledge the communion between the Spirit and the heart is to open ourselves to the wellspring of life abundant. And to live seeking a greater awareness of the union that was formed in us with the Spirit at salvation is to position ourselves to receive all that God longs to give us.

"Or do you not know that your body is a temple of the Holy Spirit within you, whom you have from God? You are not your own."

1 CORINTHIANS 6:19

1 Corinthians 6:19–20 says, *"Or do you not know that your body is a temple of the Holy Spirit within you, whom you have from God? You are not your own, for you were bought with a price."* Scripture tells us of a greater level of communion with God than we are right now experiencing. Scripture tells us that when Jesus died God tore the veil in two from top to bottom. Prior to Jesus' death, God's glory had to be contained within the temple. Now through the sacrifice of Jesus we have become the temple of God. We now have union with our Creator in the Holy Spirit.

1 Corinthians 6:17 says, *"But he who is joined to the Lord becomes one spirit with him."* Romans 8:9 says, *"You, however, are not in the flesh but in the Spirit, if in fact the Spirit of God dwells in you."* To say that God dwells in our hearts isn't just a figure of speech. If you are a believer, you have been sealed and filled with the Holy Spirit. You have constant communion with God. All that's left is to grow in your understanding of this wonderful, supernatural union you have with your heavenly Father.

The Spirit longs to reveal how near he is to you. He longs to make you more aware of his manifest presence. He longs to lead you, speak to you, fill you, satisfy you, heal you, set you free, and empower you. He longs for your heart to find freedom and security in him. He longs to be your best friend, companion, and teacher.

Take time today as you enter into guided prayer to gain a greater revelation of God's nearness. Ask him to reveal himself to you that you might know to greater depths how unified you are with him. May your time be filled with a greater measure of God's presence and love.

GUIDED PRAYER

1. Meditate on what Scripture says about the Spirit and the heart. Reflect on the communion you already have available to you with the Holy Spirit.

"Or do you not know that your body is a temple of the Holy Spirit within you, whom you have from God? You are not your own, for you were bought with a price." 1 Corinthians 6:19-20

"But he who is joined to the Lord becomes one spirit with him." 1 Corinthians 6:17

"You, however, are not in the flesh but in the Spirit, if in fact the Spirit of God dwells in you." Romans 8:9

2. Ask the Holy Spirit for a greater revelation of his nearness. Open your heart to God and receive his presence. Take notice of how close he is to your heart.

3. Rest in the presence of God. Allow a revelation of his nearness to establish within you a new reality founded on God's manifest presence.

Allow the Spirit to permeate everything you do today. Seek to live in constant awareness of his presence and love. You don't have to strive to be with God. You don't have to strive to encounter him. He is already with you. He is already in you. All that's left is for you to simply open your heart to him moment by moment. Don't live as if God is separate from you. Don't talk to him or worship him as if he is distant. Rather, live in light of Scripture and experience all the abundant life he has for you in his nearness. May your life be changed by the powerful, constant, unfailing, and wholly satisfying presence of God.

"In your presence there is fullness of joy." Psalm 16:11

Extended Reading: 1 Corinthians 6

WEEK 1

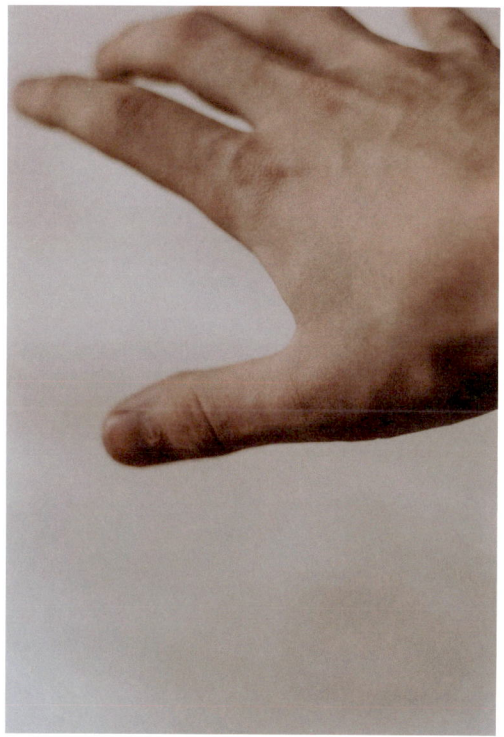
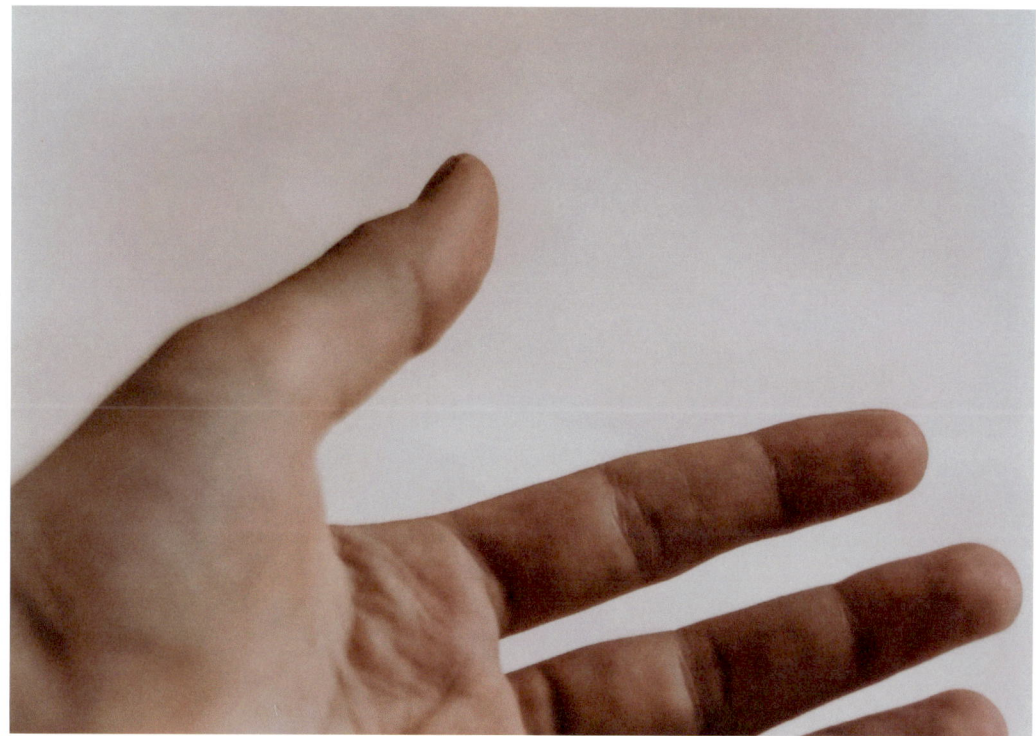

Living from the Heart

DAY 7

DEVOTIONAL

God has formed us to be creatures of the heart. He made us to live from a place of communion with him—an eternal relationship with our hearts deeply connected. And in response to the communion you have with God you can choose to live

"Trust in him at all times, O people; pour out your heart before him; God is a refuge for us."

PSALM 62:8

from your heart. You can choose with confidence to think, feel, act, and believe not just with what's logical, but with what God's Spirit is speaking to you.

Oftentimes we disclude our hearts as if they are unfounded and fickle. We stop paying attention to our emotions because we doubt their validity and value. But God formed you with emotions. And it's oftentimes your emotions that best reveal your beliefs. You don't feel stress, worry, doubt, or anger without cause. You don't experience joy, peace, passion, and purpose for no reason. Your heart is the window to your beliefs. It reveals where you've placed your trust and hope. It reveals what truly matters to you.

Psalm 62:8 says, *"Trust in him at all times, O people; pour out your heart before him; God is a refuge for us."* God longs to hear your heart. He longs for you to so trust him that you honestly and truthfully assess your heart and pour it out before him. He cares about the way you feel. He's not all right with you going through life stressed, angry, doubtful, worried, or unconfident. He wants your heart to be filled with the fruit of communion with him that you might live an expressive, passionate, and satisfied life.

Acknowledging your emotions isn't weakness. Rather, it's a sign of confidence and security that you can take an honest look at your life and assess how you're doing. Living from the heart is a crucial aspect to authentic, abundant Christianity. God doesn't want robots. He doesn't just want to influence our minds or just make us work for him. He wants all of us. He wants your mind to be renewed and your hands to be set to good work from a place of wonderful, life-giving communion with him.

Take time as you enter into guided prayer to value your heart. Assess how you've been feeling. Pour out your heart to your loving, patient, and understanding heavenly Father. And go out today in confidence that you might live openly, receptively, and passionately.

GUIDED PRAYER

1. Meditate on the importance of living from the heart.

"Trust in him at all times, O people; pour out your heart before him; God is a refuge for us." Psalm 62:8

2. Assess how you've been feeling. What's been bringing you life? What's been causing you stress, anger, or frustration. What do your emotions tell you?

3. Take some time to journal about your emotions. Pour out your heart to God on paper. Ask the Holy Spirit for revelation about anything you don't understand. Write down his responses.

Oftentimes, if we will begin our quiet time by assessing our emotions we'll be able to go deeper with God quicker. God longs for our time spent with him to be open, vulnerable, and honest. He longs to help us with those things that are truly robbing us of abundant life. And because emotions are often windows into our beliefs they are a great way to assess where we need a fresh revelation of what's true. May your life be filled with the fruit of the Spirit today as you choose to live from the heart.

Extended Reading: Psalm 62

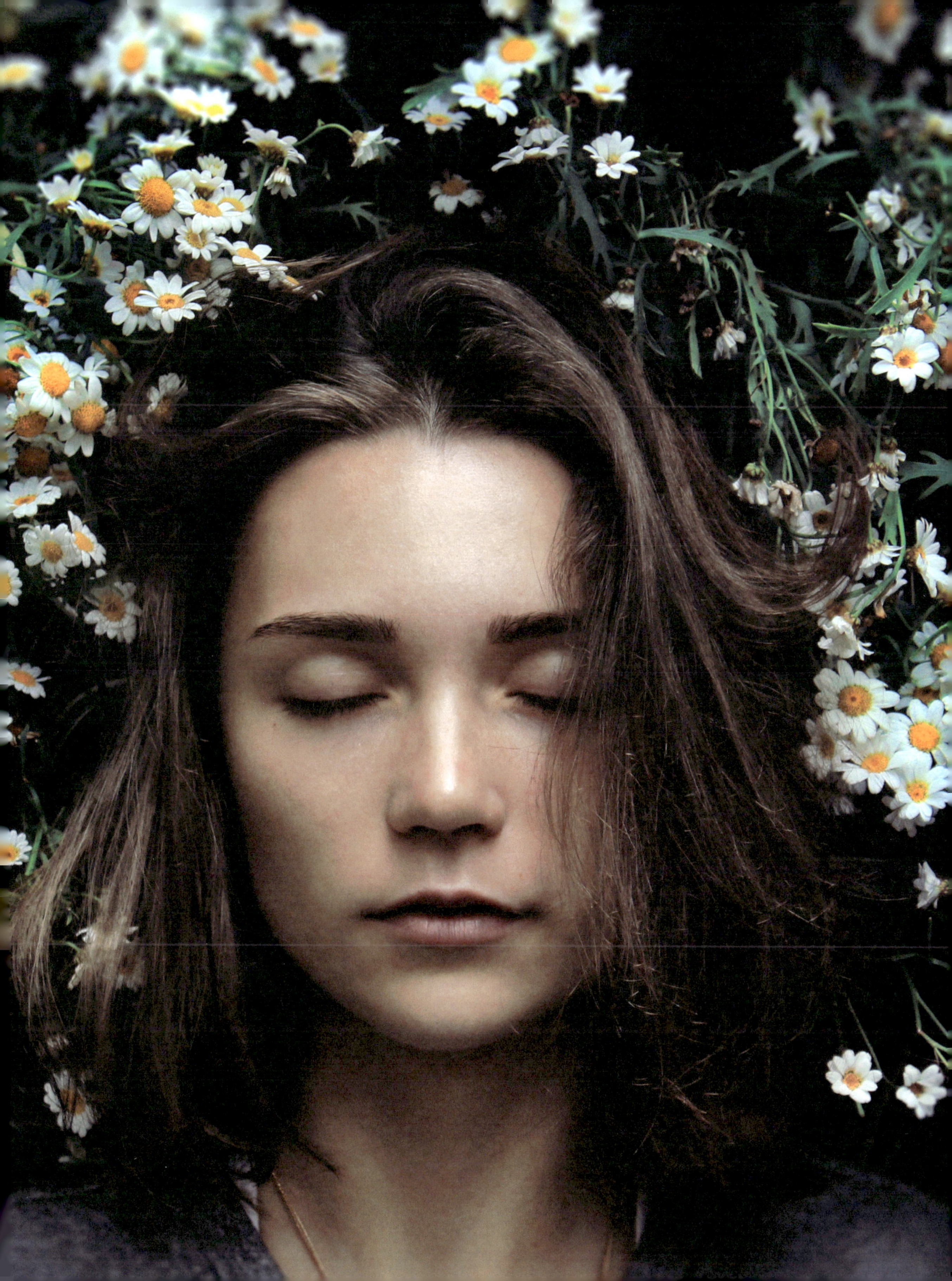

DAYS 8 - 14

Honesty

02

WEEK

"Create in me a clean heart, O God, and renew a right spirit within me." Psalm 51:10

WEEKLY OVERVIEW

Honesty is more than the words we say. It's a posture of the heart. We weren't made to try and be something we're not. God never asks us to keep up appearances. He longs for us to have the courage to be vulnerable. He longs for us to be so founded in his unconditional love that we live honestly. May you experience new levels of peace and joy this week as we discover God's heart for honesty.

Honesty is the Foundation

DAY 8

DEVOTIONAL

Deciding to live openly and honestly is foundational to experiencing fullness of life in God. God doesn't deal with our facades. He doesn't speak to, love on, heal, deliver, or empower the fake self we try and portray. Rather, he faithfully pursues who we really are, drawing us out from the walls we've built up around our hearts.

"Whoever desires to love life and see good days, let him keep his tongue from evil and his lips from speaking deceit."

1 PETER 3:10

1 Peter 3:10 says, *"Whoever desires to love life and see good days, let him keep his tongue from evil and his lips from speaking deceit."* When the Bible talks about honesty, it isn't just talking about God's heart for us not to speak lies, but also that we wouldn't believe or live out lies. In living honestly we will love life and see good days. Nothing good comes from being dishonest. There is no life in trying to appear as something we're not. Abundant life comes with communion with God, and God always meets us where we're at.

Assess your life today. Are you living honestly? Are you trying to portray yourself as something you're not? Are you deceiving yourself or looking at yourself honestly? Are you coming before God just as you are or trying to appear like you have everything together?

Honesty is at the foundation of encountering God, loving others, experiencing abundant life, and doing good, eternal works. Everything God does is about the heart. He's about that which has substance, that which is real. He's not calling you to share your "picture-perfect" life with others. He's calling you to be vulnerable with others that they would see the unconditional, grace-filled nature of relationship with God. He's not asking you to clean yourself up before you worship him or meet with him. He's asking you to come as you are that he might reveal the love he already has for you, even in your imperfections.

Take time to make honesty a core value in your life. Reflect on the importance of being open and vulnerable. Allow the Spirit to illuminate any ways in which you are valuing appearance above reality. And choose today to be who you truly are. May you find new peace and joy today as you remove the pressure of appearance.

HEART

48

GUIDED PRAYER

1. Meditate on the importance of honesty. May Scripture help you make honesty a core value.

"Whoever desires to love life and see good days, let him keep his tongue from evil and his lips from speaking deceit." 1 Peter 3:10

"For the Lord sees not as man sees: man looks on the outward appearance, but the Lord looks on the heart." 1 Samuel 16:7

"If anyone thinks he is religious and does not bridle his tongue but deceives his heart, this person's religion is worthless." James 1:26

2. Assess your heart. In what ways do you value appearance above reality? Where are you working to try and appear as something you're not. Ask the Holy Spirit to illuminate any ways in which you need to live more honestly.

3. Ask God to reveal his love for you even in your imperfections. Allow his love to fill you with the courage to be honest today. Rest in his unconditional love for you.

"But God shows his love for us in that while we were still sinners, Christ died for us." Romans 5:8

The only confidence available to us to live honestly is the unconditional love of God. Christ died for you while you were in your sin. He gave his life just to have relationship with you just as you are. Choose to receive his love. Choose to value his opinion over others' opinions. Let his love be your source over the fickle affections of people. May you find courage to be yourself today and thereby experience true freedom in your heart.

Extended Reading: 1 Peter 3

Facade

DAY 9

DEVOTIONAL

The greatest testimony you could possibly give is to have the audacity to live honestly. It takes courage to be yourself. It takes security in the unconditional love of your heavenly Father to acknowledge not just your strengths and successes, but also your weaknesses and failures. But in doing so your life will proclaim the powerful, beautiful work of God. And in doing so you will experience the peace and joy only freedom from building a facade can produce.

> *"Woe to you, scribes and Pharisees, hypocrites! For you are like whitewashed tombs, which outwardly appear beautiful, but within are full of dead people's bones and all uncleanness."*
>
> **MATTHEW 23:27**

A facade is "an outward appearance that is maintained to conceal a less pleasant or creditable reality." So often, to cover up what we know to be imperfect we devote ourselves to creating a false picture for others. We even devote so much energy to building a facade that we try and deceive ourselves. We muster up our pride and look only at what we've done well, all the while ignoring what we need help with. As a result, we spend all our time living a life apart from reality. And to live apart from reality is to live apart from the grace and love of our ever-present, wholly real Father.

In Matthew 23:27, Jesus passionately rebukes those who try and build facades: *"Woe to you, scribes and Pharisees, hypocrites! For you are like whitewashed tombs, which outwardly appear beautiful, but within are full of dead people's bones and all uncleanness."* God solely cares about the heart. He's not worried about perception. He's not worried about status or societal acceptance. He cares about what is real. He knows that any energy spent devoted to building a facade is energy you can't devote to receiving help, healing, and grace for what's real and important. He knows that all your efforts to be accepted aren't of value because the opinions of others are nothing in comparison to his unconditional love for you. And he knows that ultimately all facades will be torn down, and we will be seen and known by him for who we truly are.

God longs for you to live fully known and fully loved. He longs for you to live out a revelation of his love and grace rather than striving for affection and acceptance by building up facades. Take time to experience his love and grace today. Assess your heart and tear down your walls. May freedom burst forth in your life today as you proclaim the glory of God's grace by being who you really are.

GUIDED PRAYER

1. Reflect on the importance of living in reality. Allow Jesus' words to stir up your desire to tear down any facade you've built up.

"Woe to you, scribes and Pharisees, hypocrites! For you are like whitewashed tombs, which outwardly appear beautiful, but within are full of dead people's bones and all uncleanness." Matthew 23:27

2. Where are you striving for acceptance or affection by building up facades? Where are you portraying yourself to be something you aren't? Why are you doing it?

3. Ask the Holy Spirit for the courage to be yourself today. Tell others of your weaknesses today. Don't be afraid to be yourself with all your strengths, successes, weaknesses, and failures.

May God's grace and love empower you today as you live honestly. May you stop devoting your energy to appearances and give yourself to what's real. And in doing so may you encounter the unconditional acceptance and affection of your loving Father.

Extended Reading: Matthew 23

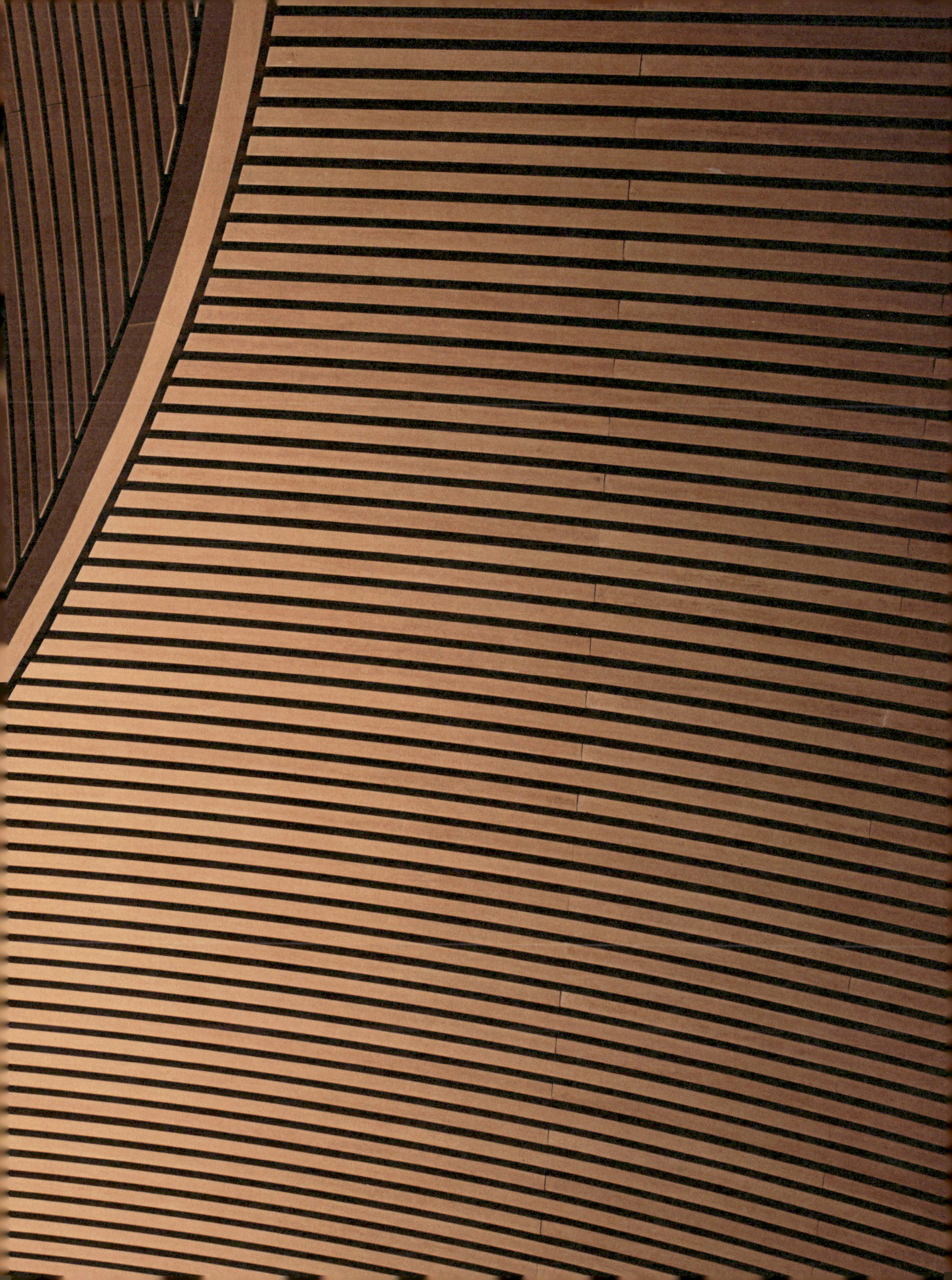

Tearing Down Walls

DAY 10

DEVOTIONAL

In order to protect our hearts from the pain and wounds of the world we both consciously and subconsciously build walls. These walls take all sorts of forms. Some walls are built for appearance so that outward beauty covers up inward brokenness. Some walls are built to be strong and tough so that pride and strength cover up inward vulnerability and self-consciousness. Some walls are built in order to blend in so that people pass us by altogether and never try to

"I always take pains to have a clear conscience toward both God and man."

ACTS 24:16

know us. Whatever wall we choose to build, one thing's for certain: the walls might guard us from harm, but they also keep us from ever experiencing true life.

Abundant life comes from being both fully known and then fully loved. We can't experience the love of God and others if we don't allow ourselves to be known. We can't experience God's grace and affection for us if we shield ourselves from him out of fear that he will see us and reject us. And whenever someone tries to love us fully we will always reject their love by saying, "If you truly knew me, you wouldn't love me." Living with walls up isn't really living; it's surviving.

God knows our pains. He knows our wounds. Psalm 34:18 says, *"The Lord is near to the brokenhearted and saves the crushed in spirit."* God is for you. He longs to be near to you and save you. But in order for you to experience the fullness of his love and healing you have to let him in. And in order for you to experience true life you have to stop trusting in your walls to protect you and start trusting in the powerful, capable hands of your loving Father.

In Psalm 57:7 David writes, *"My heart is confident in you, O God; my heart is confident"* (NLT). God is the one who protects our hearts. There is nothing we can do to fully shield ourselves from the wounds this world causes except allow our hearts to be fully open to God. Only in God can we have confidence. Only in God can we trust. And only in God will we experience true, abundant life.

Take time today to tear down your walls brick by brick. Stop placing your hope in that which can't ever truly protect you. And look to God as your great protector that you might be fully known and fully loved today. May your time of guided prayer be marked by freedom and deliverance in the Holy Spirit.

GUIDED PRAYER

1. Meditate on the importance of living without walls up.

"I always take pains to have a clear conscience toward both God and man." Acts 24:16

2. Where do you place your hope for protection? What walls have you built that you might not be truly known? In what ways are you guarding yourself?

3. Confess to God any places you've given your trust, and place your hope for protection in him alone. Journal about any walls you've built up and respond to God's promise of nearness and healing by giving him your heart.

"The Lord is near to the brokenhearted and saves the crushed in spirit." Psalm 34:18

"My heart is confident in you, O God; my heart is confident" Psalm 57:7 (NLT)

It's important to take note when you begin to build walls around your heart. Run to God when you feel insecure. Rather than building up walls that have to be torn down again, seek to live openly and honestly. May you feel God's hand of protection around your heart today.

Extended Reading: Psalm 57

WEEK 2

Fully Known

DAY 11

DEVOTIONAL

While we absolutely serve an all-knowing, omnipotent, omnipresent God, there is a stark difference between God's knowledge of everything and allowing ourselves to be known by him. To be known by God is a two-way street. It's a conscious decision to open our hearts to

> *"But if anyone loves God,
> he is known by God."*
>
> **1 CORINTHIANS 8:3**

this all-knowing God that we might experience him in even the deepest, most secret places of our lives. Galatians 4:8-9 says,

Formerly, when you did not know God, you were enslaved to those that by nature are not gods. But now that you have come to know God, or rather to be known by God, how can you turn back again to the weak and worthless elementary principles of the world, whose slaves you want to be once more?

Being known by God is the birthplace of freedom. When we allow our Creator and Savior to truly know us he brings with him all his power, love, and deliverance. Only when we allow him to know the wounds of our past do we position ourselves to receive his healing. Only when we discover that he cries, mourns, laughs, and celebrates with us will our hearts be founded on the reality of true relationship with him.

Your God doesn't just want to teach you, lead you, empower you, or use you—he wants to know you. You don't have to go through this life on your own. You don't have to process decisions, pains, relationships, or doubts on your own. You can be known by your Creator and know him. Unhindered relationship with your perfect, loving Father can be your source.

It is entirely possible to go through this life as a believer without letting God fully know you. As tragic as it may be, many Christians do it every day. We live as if God is distant from us. We live as if we don't have full access to his heart, will, love, and presence in the Holy Spirit. We live as if all Christ came to do was give us a "get out of Hell free card" rather than restore us to right relationship with the Father. And when you live fully known by God you will experience a love more sure, more real, and more transcendent than any love you've experienced.

Take time as you enter into guided prayer to truly let God know you. Open up the secret places of your heart. Tell him about your insecurities, fears, doubts, and wounds. May you find a deeper level of intimacy with your loving Father than you thought possible.

GUIDED PRAYER

1. Meditate on the importance of being known by God.

"Formerly, when you did not know God, you were enslaved to those that by nature are not gods. But now that you have come to know God, or rather to be known by God, how can you turn back again to the weak and worthless elementary principles of the world, whose slaves you want to be once more?" Galatians 4:8-9

"But if anyone loves God, he is known by God." 1 Corinthians 8:3

2. Are you living your life known? Or are you hiding pieces of your life from your heavenly Father?

3. Tell God about anything in your life that's stayed in the dark. Bring it to the light with him. Allow him to fully know you. And experience powerful freedom as he reveals the depths of his love for you.

"The spirit of man is the lamp of the Lord, searching all his innermost parts." Proverbs 20:27

Ephesians 5:8 says, *"For at one time you were darkness, but now you are light in the Lord. Walk as children of light."* You can live with confidence and joy today. When you are fully known by God and still fully accepted and loved, your heart is unshakable. God will not reject you. He has loved you at your worst. Trust in him today and experience life in the light of his presence.

Extended Reading: 1 Corinthians 13

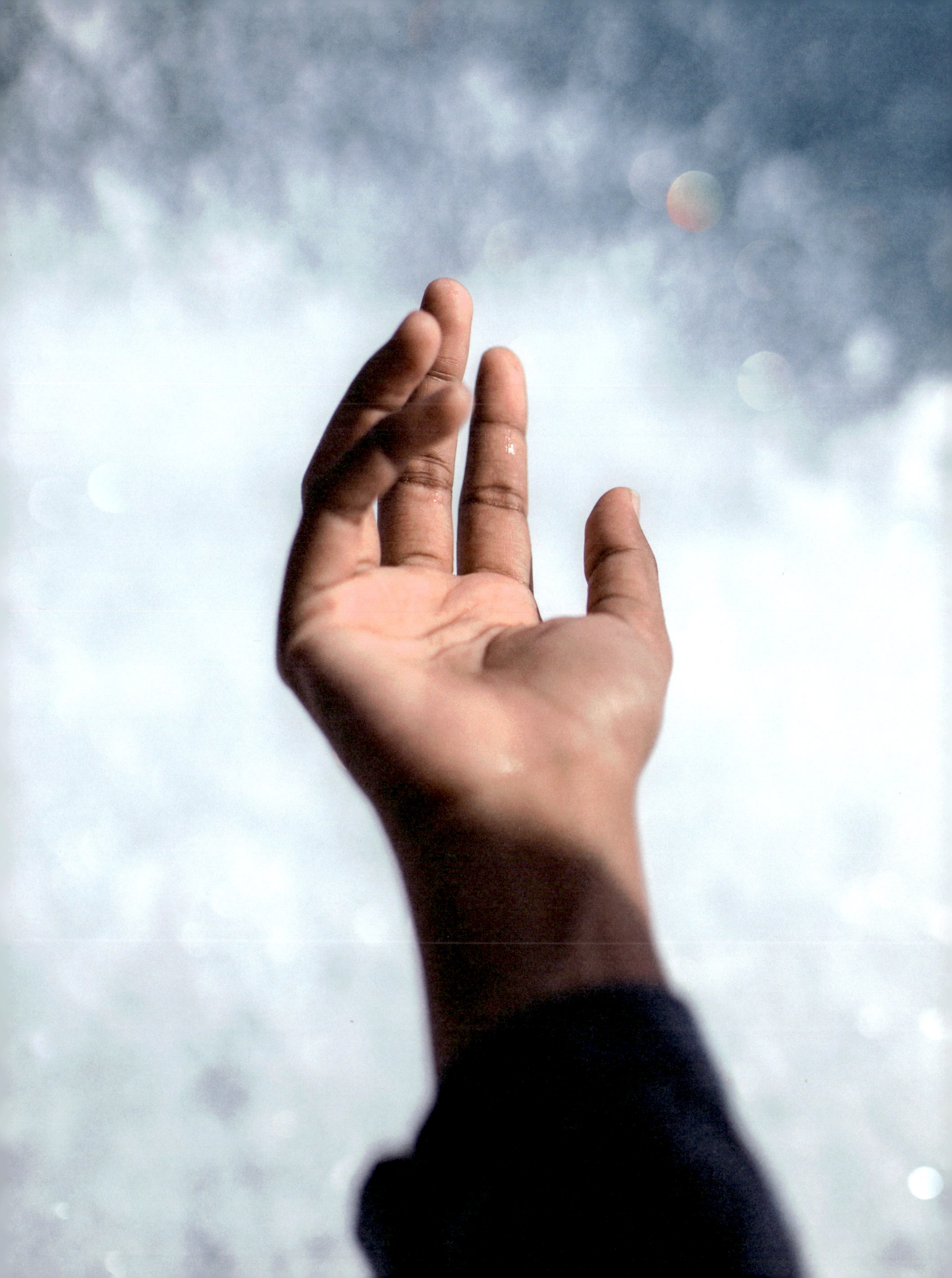

Fully Loved

DAY 12

DEVOTIONAL

The ultimate result of honesty—the reason for being fully known—is that we might be fully loved. You weren't made to live without a continuous, total revelation of God's love for you. His love is the foundation. It's the reason for being. Without his love we have nothing. And without honesty we'll never fully experience his vast wealth of affection for us.

*"For the mountains may depart and
the hills be removed, but my steadfast
love shall not depart from you."*

ISAIAH 54:10

Isaiah 54:10 is God's promise for you and me today. He says to us, *"For the mountains may depart and the hills be removed, but my steadfast love shall not depart from you."* The question today is not whether God loves us. And the question is not whether we have the ability to experience his love. Scripture commands us in Psalm 34:8, *"Oh, taste and see that the Lord is good!"* The question is whether we're receiving the love already made available to us.

You see, unless we come before God fully honest we only present part of ourselves for him to love. Unless we let him in to every area of our lives, we'll live with a separated notion of God's love. Most of us know that he loves us when we worship. We know he loves us when we serve. We've experienced his love when we engage in community, read Scripture, and pray. But do we know he loves us when we fail? Do we know he loves us when we say the wrong thing, doubt him, miss an opportunity to share the gospel, or run away from him?

God doesn't just love us part of the time. He doesn't just love us when we succeed. His love is complete and transcendent of us. He is love. He loves all the time. Romans 5:8 says, *"But God shows his love for us in that while we were still sinners, Christ died for us."* God has loved you at your worst. If he loved you enough to die for you while you were without one ounce of good, he will love you now.

If you want to experience the full depth of God's love for you, you must come to him fully. You must let him in to every part of your day. You must let him in to your past, your present, and your future. You must live out of a revelation of his unconditional love for you rather than living a works-based relationship with him.

May you encounter the fullness of God's love for you today as you enter into guided prayer. And may his love for you draw you deeper into the unhindered communion that's already available to you.

HEART

GUIDED PRAYER

1. Meditate on the unconditional nature of God's love. Allow Scripture to paint the picture of who God is rather than our limited, worldly perspective.

"No, in all these things we are more than conquerors through him who loved us. For I am sure that neither death nor life, nor angels nor rulers, nor things present nor things to come, nor powers, nor height nor depth, nor anything else in all creation, will be able to separate us from the love of God in Christ Jesus our Lord." Romans 8:37-39

2. Come before God and be fully known. Open every part of your heart to him. Ask the Holy Spirit to reveal how God wants to love you today. Journal his response.

"But if anyone loves God, he is known by God." 1 Corinthians 8:3

3. Take some time to simply receive and rest in God's love. Experience the unconditional nature of his love. Let his love lead you to a life founded on grace rather than works.

"Let us then with confidence draw near to the throne of grace, that we may receive mercy and find grace to help in time of need." Hebrews 4:16

To live by grace is to choose to believe God at his word. It's choosing to live based on Scripture over everything we've known from the world. Grace isn't found here. It's a product of heaven alone. But God has ransomed us from a life based on the ways of the world. We belong to heaven now. And we have so much more available to us than the world offers. We are totally and fully loved regardless of our weaknesses and failures. May you live out of a revelation of grace and receive God's love in every part of your day.

Extended Reading: Romans 8

Freedom in the Light

DAY 13

DEVOTIONAL

The imagery of light and darkness is used throughout Scripture as a metaphor for freedom and sin, and God and that which is without God. Jesus consistently refers to himself as the light. In reference to Jesus, Matthew 4:16 says, *"The people dwelling in darkness have seen a great light, and for those dwelling in the region and shadow of death, on them a light has dawned."* Scripture also refers to us as the light in Ephesians 5:8 saying, *"For at one time you were darkness, but now you are light in the Lord."* And in John 3:19-21, Jesus describes a freedom that comes from bringing ourselves to the light:

And this is the judgment: the light has come into the world, and people loved the darkness rather than the light because their works were evil. For everyone who does wicked things

> *"And I will lead the blind in a way that they do not know, in paths that they have not known I will guide them. I will turn the darkness before them into light, the rough places into level ground. These are the things I do, and I do not forsake them."*

ISAIAH 42:16

hates the light and does not come to the light, lest his works should be exposed. But whoever does what is true comes to the light, so that it may be clearly seen that his works have been carried out in God.

One of the worst effects of sin is the shame it brings that causes us to hide from God and others. Adam and Eve hid from God because of the shame of the first sin. And still today, even though Christ has paid the price for every sin we could ever commit, we hide ourselves from God.

God longs for us to run to him when we make a mistake. He's the father in the prodigal son story whose arms are eternally extended to us no matter what we've done. He longs to embrace us, restore us, and free us in his eternal embrace. He longs for us to step out of our shame, bring ourselves fully into his light, and be delivered from the destructive effects of our sin.

In Isaiah 42:16 God says, *"I will lead the blind in a way that they do not know, in paths that they have not known I will guide them. I will turn the darkness before them into light, the rough places into level ground. These are the things I do, and I do not forsake them."* Nothing you could do could cause your God to forsake you. He's not surprised by your sin. He knows you are dust. But he longs to embrace you in your weakness. He longs to free you from the power of darkness. You don't have to hide from him. You can come before your God honestly and live as a child of the light (Ephesians 5:8). You can experience true freedom as your sin is forgiven and times of refreshing come (Acts 3:19-20).

Take time as you enter into guided prayer to bring that which has caused you shame into the light. May you find freedom today as God reveals to you the power of his forgiveness and grace.

GUIDED PRAYER

1. Reflect on what Scripture says about light and darkness. Allow God's word to stir up your desire to bring yourself fully to the light.

"For at one time you were darkness, but now you are light in the Lord." Ephesians 5:8

"And I will lead the blind in a way that they do not know, in paths that they have not known I will guide them. I will turn the darkness before them into light, the rough places into level ground. These are the things I do, and I do not forsake them." Isaiah 42:16

2. What do you need to bring to the light? What is causing you shame?

3. Bring yourself to the light. Ask God how he feels about that which is causing you shame. Take time to receive his forgiveness and grace and rest in his love.

1 John 1:7 says, *"But if we walk in the light, as he is in the light, we have fellowship with one another, and the blood of Jesus his Son cleanses us from all sin."* When you commit yourself to walk with God throughout your day, he will guide you to the light. Jesus' blood is powerful enough to cleanse you from the inside out. There is freedom when your heart is totally and completely his. May you be set free from shame and darkness today as you live openly and honestly before the Lord your God.

Extended Reading: John 3

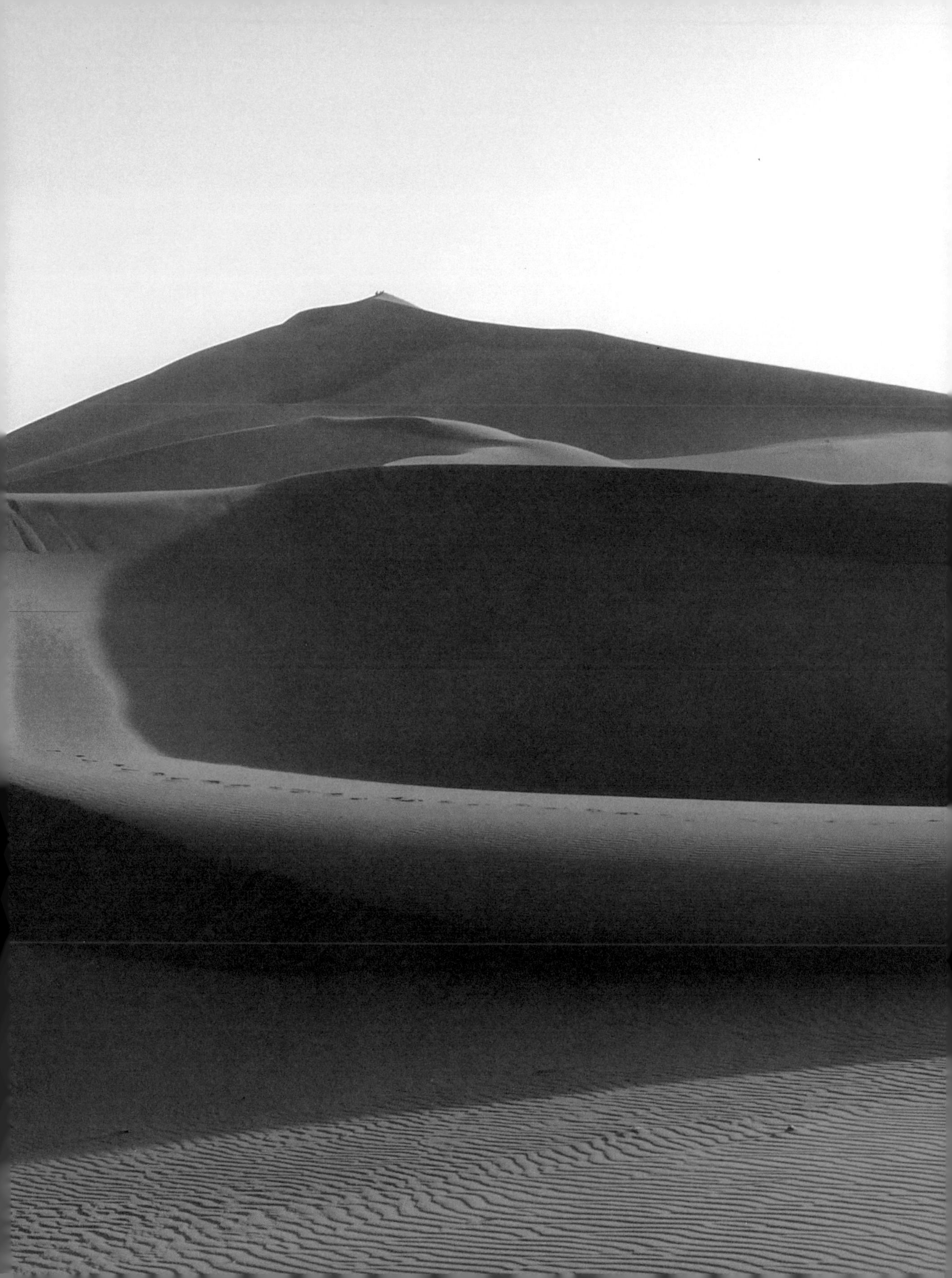

Living Honestly

DAY 14

DEVOTIONAL

There is no substitute for the peace and joy of living honestly. When you find courage from the unconditional love of your heavenly Father to truly be yourself, you alleviate yourself of the pressure and stress of keeping up appearances. And when you're free from keeping up appearances you have time and energy to devote to that which is real—that which is eternal.

> *"If anyone thinks he is religious and does not bridle his tongue but deceives his heart, this person's religion is worthless."*

JAMES 1:26

James 1:26 says, *"If anyone thinks he is religious and does not bridle his tongue but deceives his heart, this person's religion is worthless."* Did you know you were capable of deceiving your own heart? James makes an incredibly strong statement here. How could my religion be worthless if I simply tell a small lie here or there? How could a little deception in my heart make my religion null and void?

This verse illustrates just how important our hearts are to God. 1 Samuel 16:7 says, *"For the Lord sees not as man sees: man looks on the outward appearance, but the Lord looks on the heart."* Your religion is only as valuable as it is true. The parts of you that are outward, e.g., your words, actions, and appearance, are only as valuable as they are a true reflection of your heart.

James is speaking here to those who think that what they say and do defines them. He's speaking to those who believe their value and identity are wrapped up in their good works. But God flips our worldly paradigm on its head. He values actions done from the heart. He values appearances that are a reflection of the beauty in our hearts. He values words that come from a place of deep honesty and vulnerability. He values religion that is the fruit of his Spirit loving, leading, and filling our spirits.

As we close out this week on honesty, take time to truly assess whether you're deceiving your own heart. Are you looking to that which is outward to define you? Do you see yourself related to what you do, or are your actions the result of who you are in Christ? May your time be filled with the loving-kindness of your heavenly Father and clear revelation from the Holy Spirit.

HEART

GUIDED PRAYER

1. Meditate on what Scripture says about living honestly.

"If anyone thinks he is religious and does not bridle his tongue but deceives his heart, this person's religion is worthless." James 1:26

"For the Lord sees not as man sees: man looks on the outward appearance, but the Lord looks on the heart." 1 Samuel 16:7

2. Are you looking to that which is outward to define you? Do you see yourself related to what you do, or are your actions the result of who you are in Christ?

3. Take time to receive revelation of how God sees you. Let him show you how deeply he values who you already are. Let him reveal his grace and loving-kindness to you. Take time to rest in a fresh revelation of his love and grace.

To live honestly is to value what God values. Only in consistently encountering God's value of the heart can we begin to live out of who we are rather than working to become who we feel we should be. Only in seeing ourselves as God does will we value the wonderful identity we have as his sons and daughters. May your life be forever changed as you value honesty above appearance. May you find freedom and rest in the unchanging affections of your heavenly Father.

Extended Reading: James 1

DAYS 15 - 21

The posture of our hearts

03

WEEK

"The aim of our charge is love that issues from a pure heart and a good conscience and a sincere faith." 1 Timothy 1:5

WEEKLY OVERVIEW

God's goodness over our lives far exceeds anything we've experienced. We've only yet splashed around in the shallows of God's deep love and mercy. In order to dive deeper into the fullness of life available to us, we must learn how to posture our hearts. May your relationship with God be enriched this week as you position yourself to receive all your loving heavenly Father has to give.

Honesty before God

DAY 15

DEVOTIONAL

I've spent countless, exhausting hours in my fleeting life working to portray myself as a person I know I'm not. Whether in relationships with friends, family, my spouse, or God, I find myself consistently creating a facade for myself I hope others will like better than who I actually am. I feared that if I truly opened myself up to others and got rejected, I would have nothing left. If I am fully myself, will I be enough?

"And no creature is hidden from his sight, but all are naked and exposed to the eyes of him to whom we must give account."

HEBREWS 4:13

Hebrews 4:13 says, *"And no creature is hidden from his sight, but all are naked and exposed to the eyes of him to whom we must give account."* Scriptures like this used to seriously frighten me. The idea that an all-powerful, all-knowing, and perfectly holy God knew everything I had ever done was too invasive for me. If I couldn't even muster up the courage to truly be myself to man, how could I handle being *"naked and exposed"* to my heavenly Father?

It wasn't until I began experiencing the powerful, overwhelming love of my heavenly Father that these frail, false constructions began to fall apart brick-by-brick, lie after lie. The process God takes us through in unveiling our hearts represents his perfect kindness, patience, and pursuit of us. He waits for us to come before him, openly and honestly, patiently beckoning us with his love. He is perfectly accepting of us as long as we don't fake it with him. As soon as the prodigal son came home in a posture of humility and honesty, he was immediately embraced, accepted, and offered intimate relationship with his Father once again.

It's absolutely vital that we pursue honesty before God because he will not address what is not true. He will not try and help this false projection. He will not meet with that which doesn't truly exist. Brennan Manning writes in his book *Abba's Child: The Cry of the Heart for Intimate Belonging*, "The false self is frustrated because he never hears God's voice. He cannot, since God sees no one there." Thomas Merton says of the false self, "This is the man I want myself to be but who cannot exist, because God does not know anything about him" (*Merton's Place of Nowhere*, James Finley).

To be honest before God is to invite a perfectly loving, powerful, and grace-filled Father into the places of our lives that need him the most. He longs to be asked into the very wounds we work so tirelessly to cover up. He longs to heal and transform the darkest, hardest places of our hearts we've hidden into fertile soil that can bear the fruit of his Spirit. He longs for us to be fully known by him in every way that we might experience the full depths of his powerful, transformational love.

Take time in guided prayer to truly open your heart to God and be honest. Tell him your doubts, fears, and failures. Open up the parts of your past that you have worked so hard to cover up. And let his love in that you might experience healing in his powerful presence.

GUIDED PRAYER

1. Meditate on the importance of being honest before God. Ask the Holy Spirit to fill you with courage to be vulnerable before God in faith.

"And no creature is hidden from his sight, but all are naked and exposed to the eyes of him to whom we must give account." Hebrews 4:13

"Would not God discover this? For he knows the secrets of the heart." Psalm 44:21

2. Open up your heart to God and be truly honest with him. How are you feeling right now? How have you acted toward him? Ask the Holy Spirit to reveal any places of your heart that are veiled and kept in shadows.

3. Ask God to help you receive his love in the areas of your heart that are in desperate need of him. Open up to him the places of your past that have plagued you for so long. Ask him how he feels about you that you might receive healing.

"He heals the brokenhearted and binds up their wounds." Psalm 147:3

Making space in our lives to receive healing for our hearts from the Lord is a vital exercise in spiritual growth. We don't have to be plagued by the wounds from our past. We don't have to spend so much of our time and energy trying to cover up times we were genuinely hurt. The only path to growth passes through God's healing presence. He wants to address and heal that which you might feel has formed you. He wants to tear up all the work you've done to harden your heart that you might truly live healed, free, and vulnerable. Pursue healing for your heart and experience the life available to you in the power of the Holy Spirit.

Extended Reading: Psalm 103

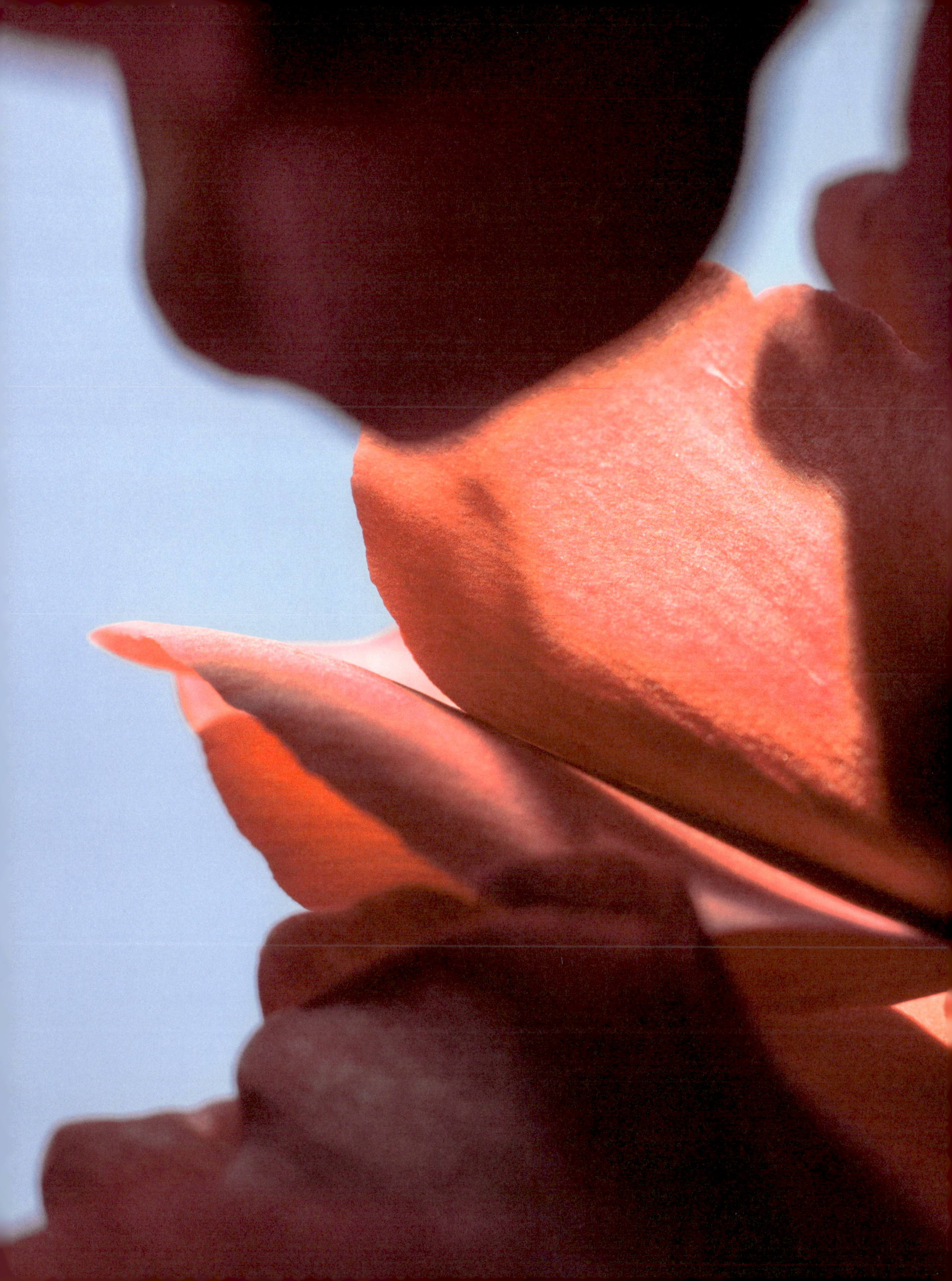

Honesty before Man

DAY 16

DEVOTIONAL

The world is right now in an identity crisis. With the global rise of social media and the Internet, we can now project ourselves to the world as anything we want. We've been given the option of only being partly known by countless people rather than really known by a few. We can attempt to fill a gap in our souls for love and relationship with the online world rather than being fully known in our strengths and weaknesses, our greatest faults and soaring successes. We're in need of an awakening of honesty.

Having an honest heart before man is the only path to experiencing true liberation from the binding opinions of others. When we work tirelessly to build up a false self so that we can receive affirmation from others, we never truly experience love. For our false self to be loved is not truly love at all because we constantly have the thought, "If they really knew me, they wouldn't love me." We have an enemy aimed at the destruction of our greatest need: truly being loved. And exaggeration, false projections, and outright lies

> *"For we aim at what is honorable not only in the Lord's sight but also in the sight of man."*
>
> **2 CORINTHIANS 8:21**

guide us exactly where our enemy wants us, into a lifestyle of never truly being known and therefore never truly being loved for who we are.

Throughout Scripture we see that wherever the Spirit is at work, the acts of confession, repentance, and truly being known to others are the result. Acts 19:18 tells us, *"Also many of those who were now believers came, confessing and divulging their practices."* And God commands us in Colossians 3:9, *"Do not lie to one another, seeing that you have put off the old self with its practices."* You see, to project a lie or exaggeration of ourselves to others is to declare that we value the opinion of man over the opinion of God. Every time we work to create a better image of ourselves, we step outside of God's grace and work for the love of man.

The path to truly being loved starts with being honest before God and man. It starts with positioning ourselves to truly be loved by God. In his book *The Furious Longing of God*, Brennan Manning describes what happens when we encounter God's furious longing for us. He says, "The praise of others will not send your spirit soaring, nor will their criticism plunge you into the pit. Their rejection may make you sick, but it will not be a sickness unto death." God longs to set us free from the emotional rollercoaster of living for the affirmation of man. God loves you where you, as you are. You don't need to strive for the fleeting, burdensome affection of people any longer. The Creator and Sustainer of the entire universe is waiting right now to pour out a love so rich and true that it will set you free from ever needing what the world has to offer.

Take time in guided prayer today to meditate on the importance of being honest with others around you. Receive the love of God and be filled with courage to be fully known. Posture your heart at a place to be truly loved by God and others for who you are. May you experience the power of true, honest love today.

HEART

GUIDED PRAYER

1. Meditate on the importance of being honest with others around you.

"Better is a poor man who walks in his integrity than a rich man who is crooked in his ways." Proverbs 28:6

"Do not lie to one another, seeing that you have put off the old self with its practices." Colossians 3:9

"Therefore, confess your sins to one another and pray for one another, that you may be healed. The prayer of a righteous person has great power as it is working." James 5:16

2. Confess to God any ways in which you've been striving for the approval of the world. Ask the Lord to overwhelm you with his love today that you might receive all you need from him. Ask him to show you how he feels about you. Receive his forgiveness.

"Repent therefore, and turn back, that your sins may be blotted out, that times of refreshing may come from the presence of the Lord." Acts 3:19-20

3. Commit yourself to being fully known today. Ask God to fill you with courage to not project yourself as better or different than you are. Ask him to help you live today as you truly are, trusting that his love is all you need.

"But God shows his love for us in that while we were still sinners, Christ died for us." Romans 5:8

"There is no fear in love, but perfect love casts out fear. For fear has to do with punishment, and whoever fears has not been perfected in love." 1 John 4:18

One of the most powerful ways to be free from creating a false self is to engage in consistent confession with fellow believers. Your spouse needs to know your sin. Healing and freedom comes from bringing what was in the dark into the light so that we might gain proper perspective and have victory. The enemy longs to keep our sins in the dark until the day that bringing them to the light will do the greatest damage to us and to God. Don't allow fear to keep you from the fullness of life God has for you. Confess your sins to others today, and ask for their help in being fully known. May you have faith that God will only ever guide you to a more abundant life. And may you receive the freedom and love that comes from truly being known today.

Extended Reading: Colossians 3

Acknowledging Our Need

DAY 17

DEVOTIONAL

The greatest place for our hearts to be is in constant acknowledgment of our need for God. Our God never forces his help on us. He never forces us to follow his perfect, pleasing will. And he never forces us into the encounters with him we were created for. But, as soon as we acknowledge our need of him, his love comes rushing in, satisfying every dry and weary place of our heart.

In Luke 10:38-42, we find one of the most important lessons in all of Scripture. The Bible says,

"Now as they went on their way, Jesus entered a village. And a woman named Martha welcomed him into her house. And she had a sister called Mary, who sat at the Lord's feet and listened to his teaching. But Martha was distracted with much serving. And she went up to him and said, "Lord, do you not care that my sister has left me to serve alone? Tell her then to help me." But the Lord answered her, "Martha, Martha, you are anxious and troubled about many things, but one thing is necessary. Mary has chosen the good portion, which will not be taken away from her."

Jesus' words here draw me to a higher calling. I long for the *"good portion"* that won't be taken away. I see here a truth I so often don't pursue. The absolute best thing I could "do for God" is to sit at his feet. The thing he most desires of me is to simply open my heart and let him love me, teach me, heal me, and be with me. Mary acknowledged her need of God and sat at the feet of Love. Mary looked to Jesus as her source, not the opinion of her sister, and got the affirmation of God himself.

How often do we allow the temporal, fleeting parts of this life to be enough? How often do we settle for so much less than what's available to us? How often do we allow the fickle affirmations of man to be enough when we can know the thoughts of our heavenly Father toward us (Psalm 139:17-18)?

Psalm 73:26 says, *"My flesh and my heart may fail, but God is the strength of my heart and my portion forever."* Let's pursue that which is lasting and truly satisfying. Let's set aside the ways of this world and spend our days living for the presence of God. Let's center our lives around Jesus. Let's acknowledge our need of God that we might receive all the love, help, healing, and transformation he longs to provide today.

Take time in guided prayer to choose the good portion and spend time at the feet of your loving Savior.

GUIDED PRAYER

1. Meditate on the importance of acknowledging your need of God.

"I am the vine; you are the branches. Whoever abides in me and I in him, he it is that bears much fruit, for apart from me you can do nothing." John 15:5

2. Where have you been self-sufficient? Where have you been allowing the things of the world to be enough?

"My flesh and my heart may fail, but God is the strength of my heart and my portion forever." Psalm 73:26

3. Cast aside the things of the world, its worries, stresses, and fears, and take time to sit at the feet of Jesus. Ask Jesus to make you aware of his nearness. Ask him to fill you with his presence. Take time to rest in his goodness.

"Seek the Lord and his strength; seek his presence continually!" 1 Chronicles 16:11

"And my God will supply every need of yours according to his riches in glory in Christ Jesus." Philippians 4:19

May Matthew 11:25-30 guide you to the rest available to you anywhere, anytime. May you experience peace that surpasses all understanding:

At that time Jesus declared, "I thank you, Father, Lord of heaven and earth, that you have hidden these things from the wise and understanding and revealed them to little children; yes, Father, for such was your gracious will. All things have been handed over to me by my Father, and no one knows the Son except the Father, and no one knows the Father except the Son and anyone to whom the Son chooses to reveal him. Come to me, all who labor and are heavy laden, and I will give you rest. Take my yoke upon you, and learn from me, for I am gentle and lowly in heart, and you will find rest for your souls. For my yoke is easy, and my burden is light."

Extended Reading: John 15

WEEK 3

91

Faith and Trust

DAY 18

DEVOTIONAL

Where we place our faith and trust is like the currency of our hearts. We have a limited amount of faith and trust to invest and real returns to gain or lose depending on where we choose to invest them. Scripture is clear that we cannot place our faith and trust in both God and the world. We cannot choose money and God as our anchors of hope. We cannot choose both the opinion of man and God's opinion. We cannot choose our own will and his. We must, moment-by-moment, choose where we will invest our limited, valuable currency of faith and trust.

"And those who know your name put their trust in you, for you, O Lord, have not forsaken those who seek you."

PSALM 9:10

If we as children of God truly believe that his word is truth, a vast reservoir of peace and joy is available to us today. The Bible is clear about what we get in return for placing our faith and trust in God alone. Jesus said in Matthew 6:30, *"But if God so clothes the grass of the field, which today is alive and tomorrow is thrown into the oven, will he not much more clothe you, O you of little faith?"* And then later in verse 34, Jesus said, *"Therefore do not be anxious about tomorrow, for tomorrow will be anxious for itself. Sufficient for the day is its own trouble."* What would it look like for us to truly have faith in God to the level that we really didn't worry about tomorrow? What kind of peace would it bring to truly place the cares, burdens, and stresses of this world squarely on the shoulders of the Almighty, all-loving God?

To go deeper into the fullness of life available to us in Jesus requires putting our faith and trust in God alone. We will never experience the peace of heaven if our hope is in this earth. We will never experience the power and help of the Holy Spirit if our hope is in our own abilities, talents, and strengths. We will never fully experience the satisfaction of truly being loved if we place our hope of affirmation in the opinions of others. The only path to truly experiencing the abundant life available to us in Jesus is placing our faith and trust in him alone.

Jeremiah 29:13 promises, *"You will seek me and find me, when you seek me with all your heart."* Choose to place your faith and trust in God alone today that you might seek him with *"all of your heart."* Place your hope in him alone for he alone is faithful. Do as 1 Peter 5:7 commands and *"Cast all your anxiety on him because he cares for you"* (NIV). You will never find a return on your investment of faith and trust in anything of the world like you will in God. God will take your faith and trust and multiply it until your life is a perfect reflection of his loving-kindness. May you find true satisfaction, peace, and joy in God today as you crown him King of your heart.

GUIDED PRAYER

1. Meditate on the importance of placing your faith and trust in God alone.

"And without faith it is impossible to please him, for whoever would draw near to God must believe that he exists and that he rewards those who seek him." Hebrews 11:6

"And those who know your name put their trust in you, for you, O Lord, have not forsaken those who seek you." Psalm 9:10

2. What have you been placing your faith and trust in other than God? What have you put your hope in? Where have you been storing up treasure on earth rather than with your Father in heaven?

"But lay up for yourselves treasures in heaven, where neither moth nor rust destroys and where thieves do not break in and steal." Matthew 6:20

3. Confess those sins to God, and place your faith and trust in him alone. Receive his love and rest in his faithful presence. Allow him to reveal his heart for you that you might know the wonders of his amazing hopes and dreams for you.

"For I know the plans I have for you, declares the Lord, plans for welfare and not for evil, to give you a future and a hope." Jeremiah 29:11

"That they should seek God, in the hope that they might feel their way toward him and find him. Yet he is actually not far from each one of us." Acts 17:27

To place your faith and trust in God alone is not to free yourself from the need to act, be responsible, and work, but rather to position yourself to receive empowerment, guidance, and grace for every action, responsibility, and work. To place our faith and trust in God alone is to humble ourselves before God as our King, Shepherd, Helper, and Provider so that all we do is done through him. May your life be filled with his loving presence, guidance, and power as you place your faith and trust in him alone.

Extended Reading: Hebrews 11

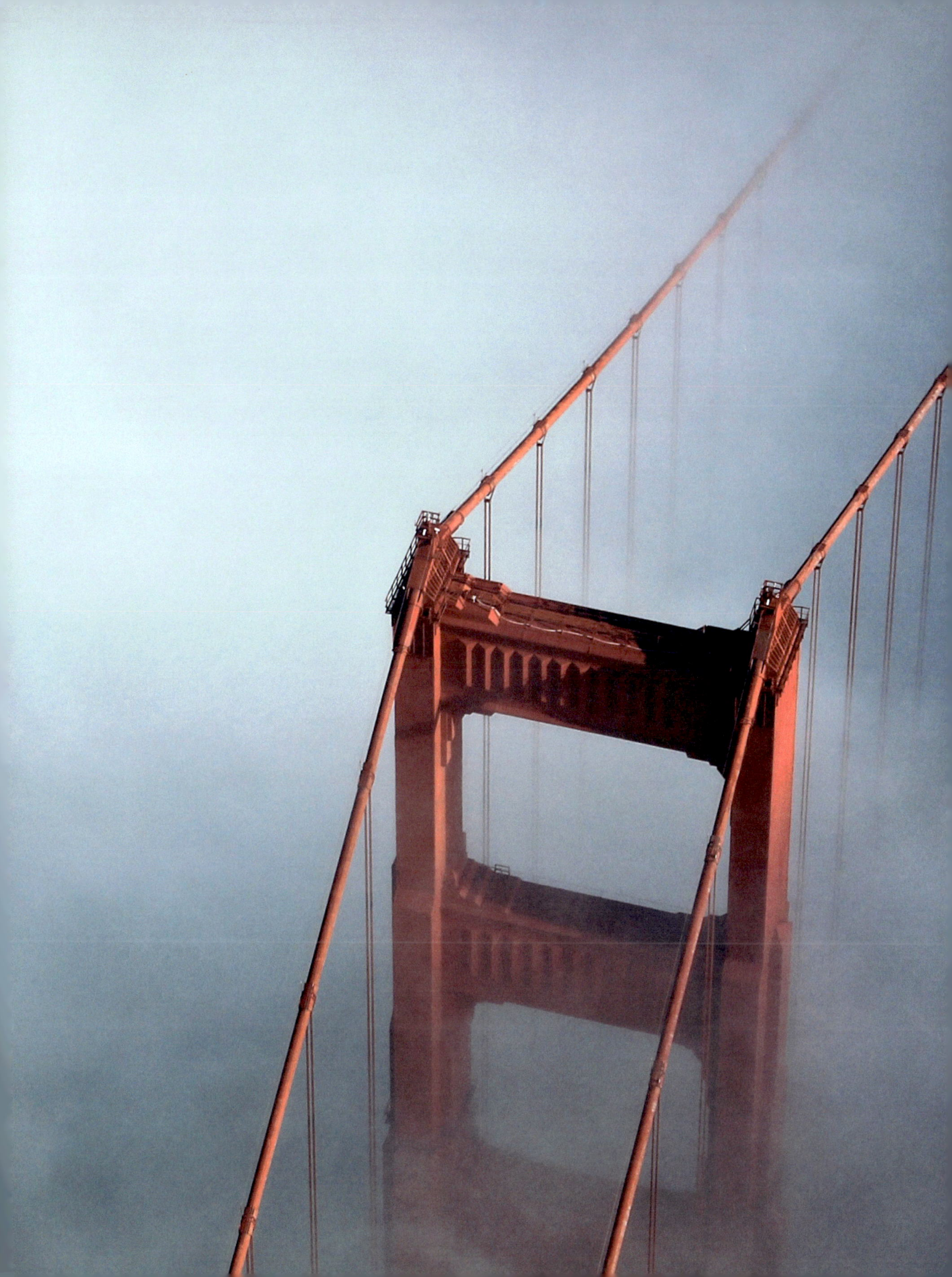

Understanding

DAY 19

DEVOTIONAL

For most believers, understanding and experience seem to be mutually exclusive. Theology and spirituality are believed to be separate, and while one might help the other, they don't belong together as one wholehearted pursuit of God. The truth is that understanding and experience couldn't be more intertwined. In fact, one does not truly exist without the other. To experience God is to have understanding. To understand God is to experience. It's for this reason Jesus said in John 4:23-24, *"But the hour is coming, and is now here, when the true worshipers will worship the Father in spirit and truth, for the Father is seeking such people to worship him. God is spirit, and those who worship him must worship in spirit and truth."*

God longs for us to know him in spirit and truth, in experience and understanding. I can't truly know someone by just reading a book about them. I can't say that I know C. S. Lewis, Martin Luther, or Dietrich Bonhoeffer just because I've read a biography or some of their works. It is the same with God. Scripture is intended to give us understanding about God and guide us into a true relationship with him. Its words are intended to be an avenue to the Author who wrote them. And if we will adopt a perspective of gaining as much understanding about our heavenly Father as possible in order to know him more, Scripture will become a priceless resource to our lives we cannot do without.

"The Lord is near to all who call on him, to all who call on him in truth."

PSALMS 145:18

Having understanding about the God we're pursuing is absolutely vital to going deeper. Psalm 145:18 tells us, *"The Lord is near to all who call on him, to all who call on him in truth."* Isaiah 26:3 says, *"You keep him in perfect peace whose mind is stayed on you, because he trusts in you."* And Jesus commands us in Matthew 22:37 to *"love the Lord your God with all your . . . mind."* Your mind is the gateway to your heart. If you believe lies about who you are or who God is, you will never seek him fully or properly. If you don't know of his goodness, faithfulness, and nearness promised to you by Scripture, you'll never have a reason to pursue truly knowing God.

God longs to guide you in a process of daily renewing your mind through Scripture. The Holy Spirit longs to help and teach you the truth of Scripture that you might know the God you serve. If you will commit yourself to a process of renewing your mind, new avenues will be created from your understanding to experience. If you will truly love the Lord by giving him your understanding to be molded and transformed, the truth of his love for you will flood from your mind to the untouched, dry, and weary places in your life. Commit to growing in your understanding of the Lord today that you might grow in your relationship with your loving, near, heavenly Father.

GUIDED PRAYER

1. Meditate on the importance of worshipping God in spirit and truth.

"But the hour is coming, and is now here, when the true worshipers will worship the Father in spirit and truth, for the Father is seeking such people to worship him. God is spirit, and those who worship him must worship in spirit and truth." John 4:23-24

"You keep him in perfect peace whose mind is stayed on you, because he trusts in you." Isaiah 26:3

2. In what ways have you been pursuing experience or understanding as if they are mutually exclusive? In what ways have you allowed a head knowledge of God or an experience of God to be enough?

3. Ask the Holy Spirit to reveal to you what it's like to truly pursue God in spirit and in truth. Ask him what it's like to live your life where understanding and experience are never separated. Rest in his presence and commit yourself to knowing God in every part of your life.

"The Lord is near to all who call on him, to all who call on him in truth." Psalms 145:18

"When the Spirit of truth comes, he will guide you into all the truth, for he will not speak on his own authority, but whatever he hears he will speak, and he will declare to you the things that are to come." John 16:13

God is after redemption and transformation in every part of our lives. Our spirit, soul, and body are not separated as if we can work on one part without developing the others. Our understanding affects both our hearts and bodies. Our emotions are impacted directly by our thoughts. And our bodies carry the weight of our stress or joy. To truly be transformed by God is to invite him into every facet of ourselves and allow his love to do a mighty and necessary work. May you experience the fullness of joy and redemption today as you invite God to transform every part of your life.

Extended Reading: John 16

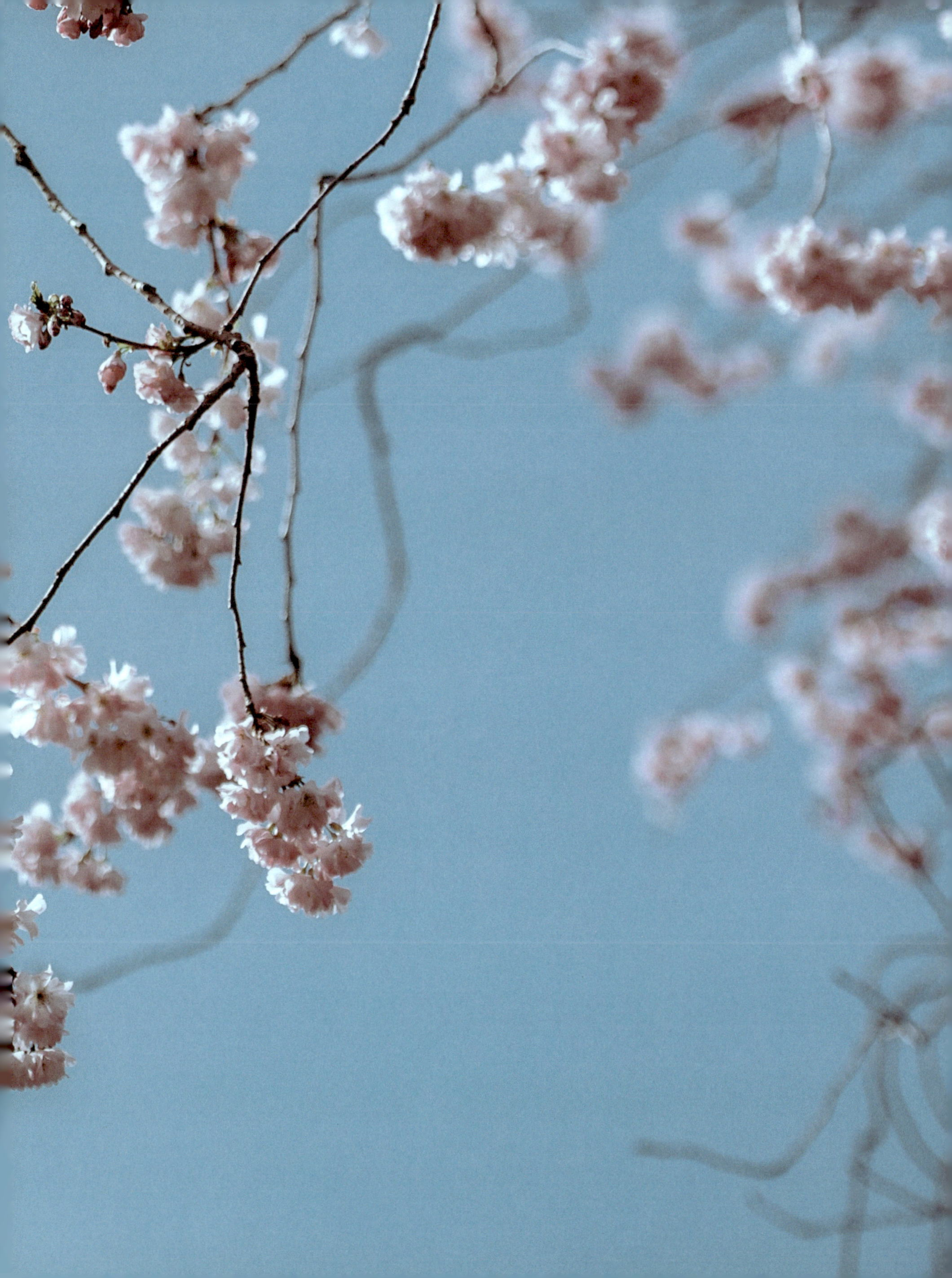

Surrender

DAY 20

DEVOTIONAL

Jesus makes an important and paradoxical statement in Matthew 10:39: *"Whoever finds his life will lose it, and whoever loses his life for my sake will find it."* What does it look like to lose your life for his sake? How is it possible to find life as the result of losing it? You and I are only truly living to the degree that we've surrendered our

> *"Whoever finds his life will lose it, and whoever loses his life for my sake will find it."*

MATTHEW 10:39

lives to Jesus. True life is eternal, kingdom-based, and fueled by the love of God. Life apart from God is fleeting and meaningless. It's for this reason Solomon in Ecclesiastes 1:14 says, *"I have seen everything that is done under the sun, and behold, all is vanity and a striving after wind."*

We have opportunity every day to lay our lives down at the feet of Jesus in response to his great love that we might experience the abundant life only he can give. Surrender positions our hearts to receive the incredible reward of being fully God's. God won't force his blessings on us. He won't force his presence or his love. He patiently draws us near, hoping that in response to his overwhelming affections we will lay down our lives that we might experience all the wonders he has in store for us.

Humbling ourselves before God as our King, Creator, and Sustainer is absolutely vital in going deeper. Pride so often stands in the way of God's conditional promises. Scripture is clear in James 4:6, *"God opposes the proud, but gives grace to the humble."* Promises like *"Seek first the kingdom of God and his righteousness, and all these things will be added to you"* found in Matthew 6:33 require a level of humility and surrender most aren't willing to give.

We often associate humility with weakness when in reality declaring our weakness before an Almighty God is the only posture of strength we can take. It's for this reason that Paul says in 2 Corinthians 11:30, *"If I must boast, I will boast of the things that show my weakness."* When we humble ourselves before God and surrender, we position ourselves to receive all the abundance of help, power, guidance, and love we could ever need.

God is an endless ocean of love, help, healing, and power. The Holy Spirit who dwells within you longs to empower you with everything you need to truly live in the fullness of life available to you. If you will choose to lay down your life in surrender to God's plans, purposes, truth, and perfect will, you will experience a life unlike anything you've known. Take time today to lose your life that you may find it in God. Cast aside all pride and selfish ambition that you might pursue the wonderful, abundant life of one submitted to an Almighty, omnipotent, omnipresent, and fully loving Father.

GUIDED PRAYER

1. Meditate on the need for surrender in fully pursuing God.

"Whoever finds his life will lose it, and whoever loses his life for my sake will find it." Matthew 10:39

"But he gives more grace. Therefore it says, 'God opposes the proud, but gives grace to the humble.'" James 4:6

"Blessed are the poor in spirit, for theirs is the kingdom of heaven." Matthew 5:3

2. In what ways have you been allowing pride, fear, or selfish ambition to keep you from fully surrendering to God? In what ways have you been seeking glory for yourself?

3. Lay your life down at the feet of your good and loving Savior that you might experience the fullness of his love, grace, and affection for you. Rest at the feet of Jesus. Choose the good portion today rather than spending all your energy seeking fleeting admiration and temporal possessions.

"Now as they went on their way, Jesus entered a village. And a woman named Martha welcomed him into her house. And she had a sister called Mary, who sat at the Lord's feet and listened to his teaching. But Martha was distracted with much serving. And she went up to him and said, 'Lord, do you not care that my sister has left me to serve alone? Tell her then to help me.' But the Lord answered her, 'Martha, Martha, you are anxious and troubled about many things, but one thing is necessary. Mary has chosen the good portion, which will not be taken away from her.'" Luke 10:38-42

While surrender in the world results in defeat, surrender to God brings ultimate victory. When we stop pursuing our own glory and worldly acclamations, we begin building up treasure in heaven that will never be taken away from us. God's plans for us are infinitely better than anything we could do on our own. His heavenly rewards for us vastly outweigh any sense of earthly accomplishments. Surrendering our lives completely to God releases us from the constraints of this world that we might live for the kingdom that will never end. May your life be completely wrapped up in the goodness of your loving Savior.

Extended Reading: James 4

Gaining Spiritual Eyes

DAY 21

DEVOTIONAL

In order to go deeper in God, we must allow him to open the eyes of our hearts to see him as he truly is. So often we settle in our relationship with him for that which can only be seen with our physical eyes. We settle for community apart from unity in the Spirit, God's word apart from revelation from the Spirit, and look to "open" or "closed" doors as our guide rather than making space to ask for the Holy Spirit's leadership. It's time for us as the body of Christ to truly live in the fullness of relationship afforded to us by his sacrifice. It's for this reason, in Ephesians 1:16-19, Paul told the Church in Ephesus,

"Having the eyes of your hearts enlightened, that you may know what is the hope to which he has called you, what are the riches of his glorious inheritance in the saints."

EPHESIANS 1:18

I do not cease to give thanks for you, remembering you in my prayers, that the God of our Lord Jesus Christ, the Father of glory, may give you the Spirit of wisdom and of revelation in the knowledge of him, having the eyes of your hearts enlightened, that you may know what is the hope to which he has called you, what are the riches of his glorious inheritance in the saints, and what is the immeasurable greatness of his power toward us who believe.

We need the *"eyes of our hearts"* to be enlightened today. We need the Holy Spirit to come and do a mighty work that we might no longer live only for that which is seen, but by faith pursue the unseen. Hebrews 11:1 says, *"Now faith is the assurance of things hoped for, the conviction of things not seen."* God longs for us to pursue the deeper things of him in faith. He longs for us to grow in our relationship with the Holy Spirit and learn to live life with his presence, leadership, voice, and love as the foundation for everything we do.

To live only by the things we can physically see is to live only for that which is temporal and fleeting. Psalm 101:3 says, *"I will not set before my eyes anything that is worthless. I hate the work of those who fall away; it shall not cling to me."* God has worthwhile work in store for us. He has a plan to bring heaven to earth through our lives every day. But in order to make an impact on eternity we must be able to see and know the heart of God. We must become increasingly aware of how God feels and what he wants to do moment-by-moment.

Growing in our relationship with the Holy Spirit is the foundation of seeking the deeper things of God. Learning to live by and with him is the only way to advance his kingdom. Take time in guided prayer today to ask the Holy Spirit to open the eyes of your heart. Ask him to guide you into a deeper and more connected relationship with him. And choose today to pursue a life marked by deep connection with your heavenly Father and powerful works of his Spirit.

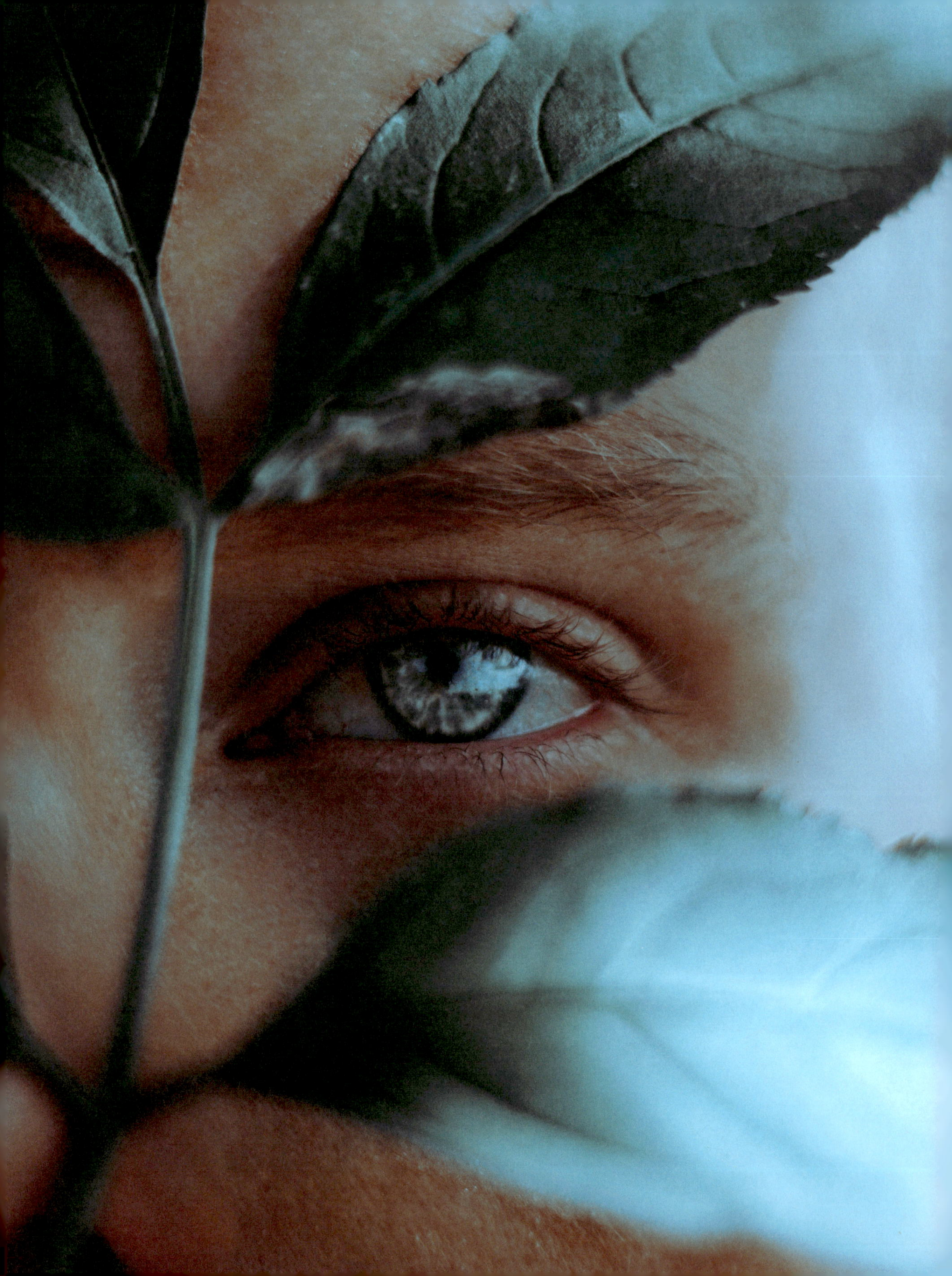

GUIDED PRAYER

1. Ask the Holy Spirit to open the eyes of your heart. Meditate on Scripture and take time to rest in his presence.

"Having the eyes of your hearts enlightened, that you may know what is the hope to which he has called you, what are the riches of his glorious inheritance in the saints." Ephesians 1:18

"Then Elisha prayed and said, 'O Lord, please open his eyes that he may see.' So the Lord opened the eyes of the young man, and he saw, and behold, the mountain was full of horses and chariots of fire all around Elisha." 2 Kings 6:17

"The hearing ear and the seeing eye, the Lord has made them both." Proverbs 20:12

2. Where have you been doing life apart from connectivity to the Spirit? Where have you been living temporally instead of for eternity?

"And I will ask the Father, and he will give you another Helper, to be with you forever, even the Spirit of truth, whom the world cannot receive, because it neither sees him nor knows him. You know him, for he dwells with you and will be in you." John 14:16-17

"Do not lay up for yourselves treasures on earth, where moth and rust destroy and where thieves break in and steal, but lay up for yourselves treasures in heaven, where neither moth nor rust destroys and where thieves do not break in and steal. For where your treasure is, there your heart will be also." Matthew 6:19-21

3. Ask the Holy Spirit to help you live connected to him today.

"Be filled with the Spirit." Ephesians 5:18

"For in one Spirit we were all baptized into one body—Jews or Greeks, slaves or free—and all were made to drink of one Spirit." 1 Corinthians 12:13

"Or do you not know that your body is a temple of the Holy Spirit within you, whom you have from God? You are not your own" 1 Corinthians 6:19

Jesus promised us in Matthew 7:7, *"Ask, and it will be given to you; seek, and you will find; knock, and it will be opened to you."* When we seek all the blessings God has to give such as being loved, being known, being provided for, and being filled with the Spirit, we can know that we will find what we seek. The door to going deeper in God will always be opened whenever we come to it and knock. God will never withhold himself from us when we purely desire more of him. Have faith today in the goodness of your heavenly Father and pursue the deeper things of him that you might live in greater union with him today.

Extended Reading: Ephesians 1

DAYS 22 - 28

Sharing God's heart

04

WEEK

"By this all people will know that you are my disciples, if you have love for one another." John 13:35

WEEKLY OVERVIEW

In response to knowing the heart of God we are called to share the wonders of his invisible nature with a world in desperate need of him. God has chosen to use us to reveal himself. He's filled us with the Spirit and empowered us to proclaim the good news of salvation and restored relationship with our Creator. May you discover this week that you were made to share God's heart. And may you find joy and passion in God's longing to use you in powerful and unique ways.

God wants to Use You

DAY 22

DEVOTIONAL

Ephesians 2:8-10 says: *For by grace you have been saved through faith. And this is not your own doing; it is the gift of God, not a result of works, so that no one may boast. For we are his workmanship, created in Christ Jesus for good works, which God prepared beforehand, that we should walk in them.*

"For we are his workmanship, created in Christ Jesus for good works, which God prepared beforehand, that we should walk in them."

EPHESIANS 2:10

God's grace is meant to be our catalyst to living passionate lives that bear fruit of eternal value. You aren't meant to go through the motions. You weren't created to live a normal life whose impact only lasts for this life. God in his grace and love has called you to more. You were made for a life of deep and lasting impact. You were made to share God's heart with the world.

It can be difficult to understand God's heart in wanting to use us. For some, we write ourselves off as too sinful, weak, selfish, or inept to be used by God. For others, we view God as a taskmaster who wants to use us solely for his motives. Still others of us believe that serving God is less fun, less fulfilling, and far stranger than anything we'd like to do. We're fine with a God who would give us a "get out of hell free card," but that's about as far as we'd like him to go in relationship with him.

The truth is that your life will never be fulfilling until you allow God to use you. Ephesians 2:9 is clear that you were *"created in Christ Jesus for good works."* You won't find fulfillment in anything besides the work of God because it's not what you were made for. Material possessions apart from the provision of God become more like weights tying us down to the cares and ways of the world than sources of satisfaction. Spending your life working to become successful, appreciated, and loved in the world's eyes is more like a treadmill than a path to abundant life. If you want to live an abundant life you have to allow God to use you.

God longs to use you because he loves you. He's not selfish. He doesn't need your help. He wants to work with you. He wants your life to matter. He wants you to have eternal reward for the things you do here on earth because he's a good Father who longs to give good gifts to his children. He wants you to stop segregating your life into "God time" and "me time" and start living in continual communion with him. He wants your time at work, with friends, at church, driving, resting, relaxing, and having fun to be filled with the fullness of life that comes from doing life with him.

Take time in guided prayer to discover God's heart to use you. May your time in prayer be filled with a revelation of God's goodness, grace, and loving desire to co-labor with you.

GUIDED PRAYER

1. Meditate on God's desire to use you. Find your true identity, not in the way you've lived up to this point, but in the unshakable truth of Scripture.

"For by grace you have been saved through faith. And this is not your own doing; it is the gift of God, not a result of works, so that no one may boast. For we are his workmanship, created in Christ Jesus for good works, which God prepared beforehand, that we should walk in them." Ephesians 2:8-10

"[Jesus] gave himself for us to redeem us from all lawlessness and to purify for himself a people for his own possession who are zealous for good works." Titus 2:14

2. How do you feel about being used by God? What in your heart needs to come into alignment with the truth that you were made for good works of eternal value? Lay down any hindrances at the feet of Jesus in confession.

3. Ask God how he wants to use you today. Ask him for a specific way you can reveal his heart to others. Journal his response. Take time to rest in his presence that you would find courage and faith in the reality of God's nearness.

Learning to do good works is a lifelong pursuit. God has grace for you today. He has love and compassion for you in these moments. But he longs to meet you where you are that he might lead you to a more fruitful and abundant life. Allow God to transform your heart. Let him into every part of you that your life would be flooded with his grace and mercy. Allow him to discipline you, change you, and speak new identity into you. May you find joy and passion today as you allow God to use you in powerful, eternal ways.

Extended Reading: Ephesians 2

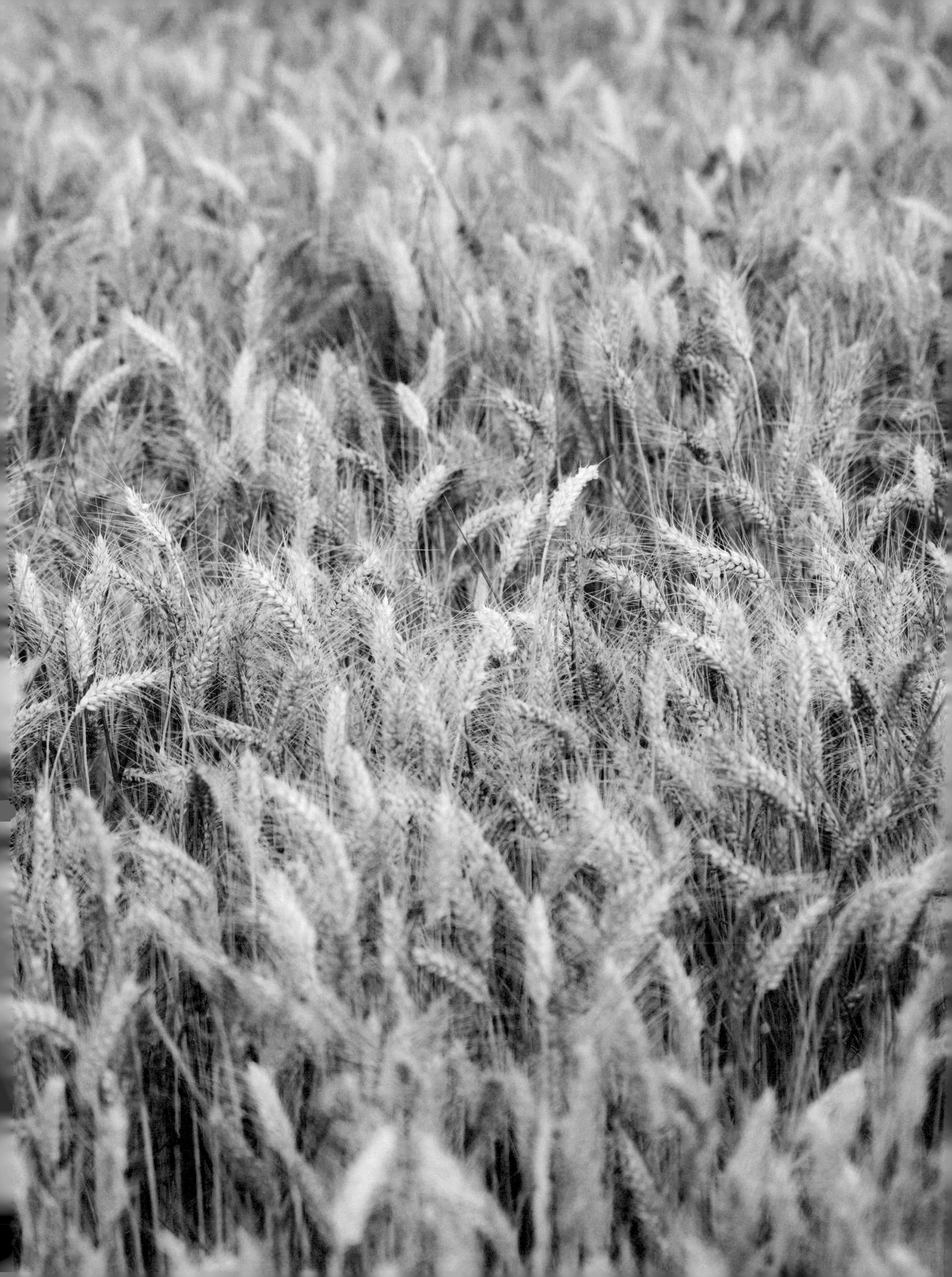

DEVOTIONAL

God is calling you and me to a lifestyle of joining him where he is already at work. Foundational to co-laboring with God is acknowledging that he is in constant pursuit of humanity. There is nowhere you can go that God won't be. There is no one you could talk to whom God doesn't already see, love relentlessly, and have amazing plans for.

Sharing God's heart begins and ends with his grace. His grace empowers us to step outside of ourselves and love others. In grace he pursues us, even in our sin. Grace sent Jesus to die for us that we might have salvation through him. And it's by grace we receive that free gift of salvation.

It's important to understand God's grace because without it we work in vain. If we operate under the perspective that salvation, healing, deliverance, and freedom for others hinges on our ability or our mercy, we will achieve nothing. But when we understand that we are merely carriers of God's heart and fellow recipients of God's lavish grace, we work from a place of power and truth.

1 Timothy 2:3-4 says, *"This is good, and it is pleasing in the sight of God our Savior, who desires all people to be saved and to come to the knowledge of the truth."* And Philippians 2:13 says, *"It is God who works in you, both to will and to work for his good pleasure."* You are not called to go off on your own into the darkness. God doesn't just meet you when you read Scripture or spend time with him and then send you off to do his will. He is always with you. He is always available to you. And he always longs to empower you.

Cultivate a lifestyle of seeing where God is at work that you might co-labor with him. Ask the Holy Spirit for eyes to see the way he is pursuing people. Ask him for his heart for your friends, family, co-workers, and those you might only encounter once. God's most likely not asking you to drop everything and move to an unreached people group right this moment. Instead, he's asking you to be used by him to minister to others you encounter in your daily rhythms of life.

Meet God where he's already at work today and seek to share his heart with a world that desperately needs to know a God who passionately pursues them.

GUIDED PRAYER

1. Meditate on the truth that God is already at work. Allow Scripture to change the way you see co-laboring with God.

"This is good, and it is pleasing in the sight of God our Savior, who desires all people to be saved and to come to the knowledge of the truth." 1 Timothy 2:3-4

"It is God who works in you, both to will and to work for his good pleasure." Philippians 2:13

2. Ask God where he is already at work around you. Ask him to bring to mind a person or a group of people whom you can minister to today.

3. Ask him how he is already at work. Ask him for a revelation of what you can do to see his kingdom advanced through your life today. Ask him for specific ways you can love others well. Journal his response and pray to receive courage and empowerment by the Holy Spirit.

Healing didn't happen in Scripture because a disciple had a greater level of mercy or compassion, but because a disciple chose to co-labor with God where he was already at work. God is constantly loving, beckoning, and drawing everyone you know to himself. And he will work through you if you seek to join with him in his purposes. If you want to live a life of purpose that has eternal value, you need not look any farther than the faces of those you see every day. May you love others as God does. May you show mercy and compassion in response to God's mercy and compassion. And may God's kingdom come to earth around you today as you minister with God.

Extended Reading: Philippians 2

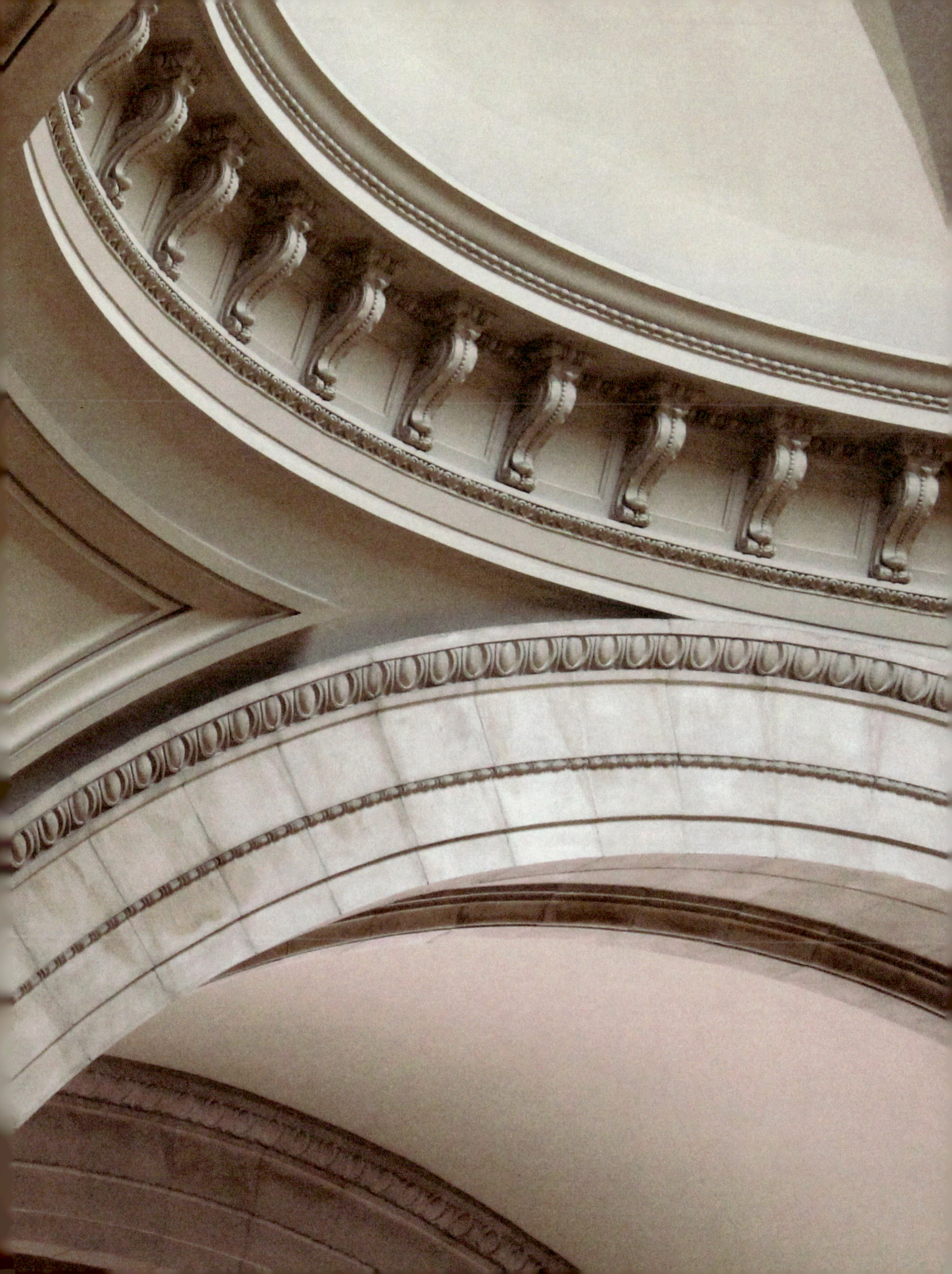

God's Glory

DAY 24

DEVOTIONAL

To declare the glory of God is to put all things in their proper place. Chaos and struggle are always the result of humanity trying to gain glory for ourselves. God alone is worthy. God alone was made to be above all else. And God alone can handle the weight of receiving glory.

"So, whether you eat or drink, or whatever you do, do all to the glory of God."

1 CORINTHIANS 10:31

1 Corinthians 10:31 says, *"So, whether you eat or drink, or whatever you do, do all to the glory of God."* We were made to declare the glory of God. We were made to proclaim through word and deed the majesty, splendor, and worthiness of the God of heaven and earth.

Proclaiming God's glory to the world always begins by taking a look at our own hearts. We can't declare that God is above every other name if we're still on the throne of our hearts. We can't proclaim his excellencies and then seek to gain success, approval, and affirmation from others. Declaring God's glory starts with our own humility. It begins with living a life of sacrifice to the one who's given up everything for us.

When we remove ourselves from the throne of our own hearts we are set free to magnify Jesus. It's when we set our eyes on our Savior King that we are freed from the weights and pressures that come from living selfishly. And in this freedom we find the life we were always meant for—a life of continual, incredibly satisfying worship.

In Revelation 19:6-8 we see a beautiful picture of heaven at the marriage supper of the Lamb. At this feast a great multitude cries out saying:

Hallelujah! For the Lord our God the Almighty reigns. Let us rejoice and exult and give him the glory, for the marriage of the Lamb has come, and his Bride has made herself ready; it was granted her to clothe herself with fine linen, bright and pure.

One day all of creation will see Jesus for who is and give him the glory he is due. One day everything will be set right, and we will discover the abundant life that comes from living for God's glory alone. But you have an opportunity to give God glory today and lead others to do the same. You have an opportunity to live with your eyes set on heaven and experience the abundant life that's already available to you. Choose today to place God on the throne of your heart and live a lifestyle of worshipping your worthy King. May your time of guided prayer be filled with a revelation of Jesus' worthiness and an empowering to declare his glory in all you do.

GUIDED PRAYER

1. Meditate on the glory of God. Allow Scripture to fill you with a desire to place God on the throne of your heart and live for his glory.

"Therefore God has highly exalted him and bestowed on him the name that is above every name, so that at the name of Jesus every knee should bow, in heaven and on earth and under the earth, and every tongue confess that Jesus Christ is Lord, to the glory of God the Father." Philippians 2:9-11

"For from him and through him and to him are all things. To him be glory forever. Amen." Romans 11:36

2. Is Jesus enthroned upon every part of your heart today? Are there any areas in your life that you are living for your own glory—to build your own kingdom? Take time to confess those areas and receive God's forgiveness and grace.

3. Ask God how you can declare his glory on the earth today. How can you live to see Jesus lifted up and seen for who he truly is? How can you lead others into a lifestyle of worship?

God doesn't want glory to satisfy some selfish need. He knows that he alone can handle a throne. He alone can handle adoration and worship. And when he is magnified it is absolutely the best thing for all of creation. It's for this reason Solomon writes in Psalm 72:19, *"Blessed be his glorious name forever; may the whole earth be filled with his glory! Amen and Amen!"* May the prayer of Solomon be our prayer today as we seek to glorify God in all we do.

Extended Reading: Psalm 8

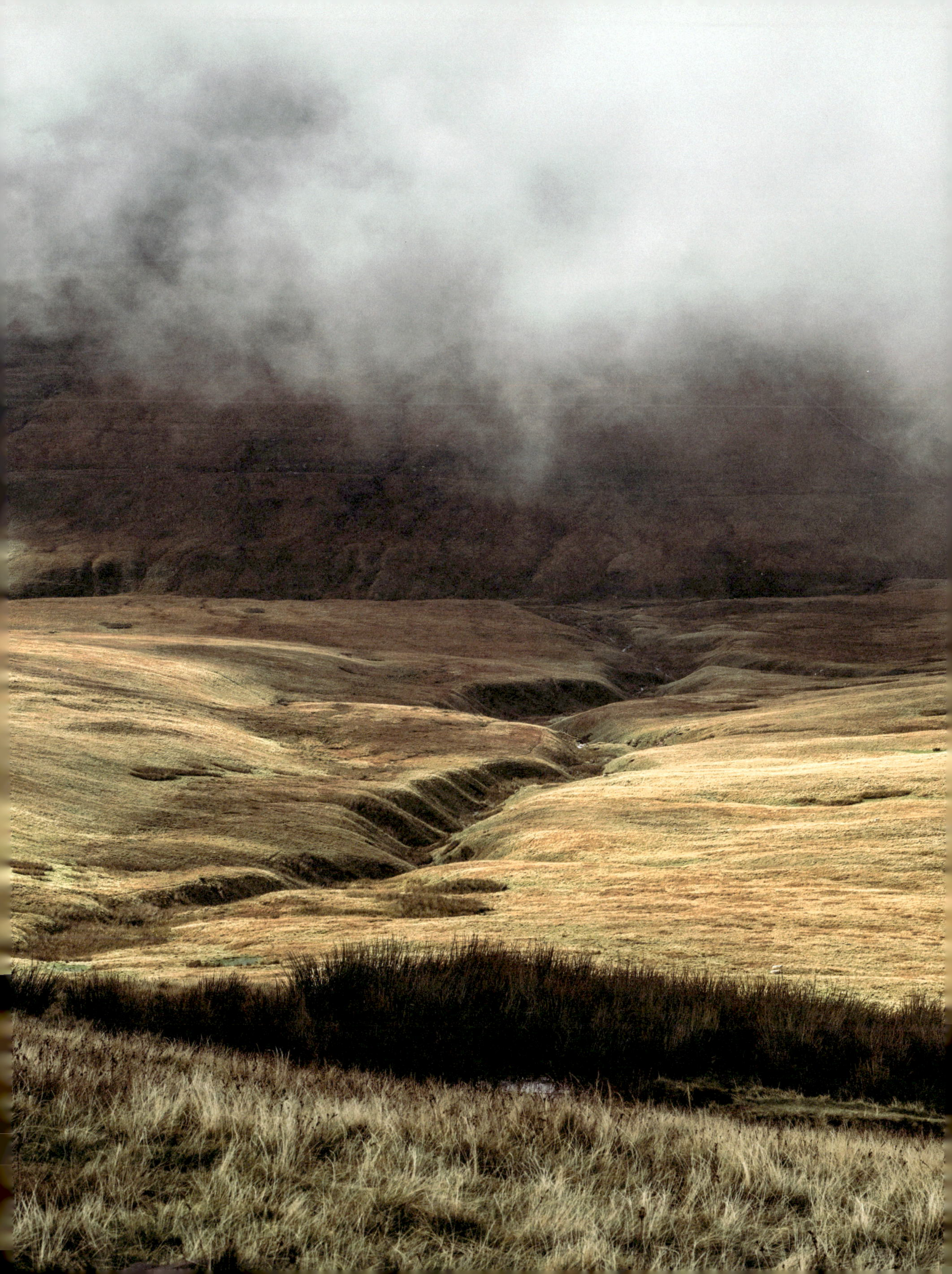

DEVOTIONAL

Jesus' teaching on salt and light in the Sermon on the Mount is one of my favorite passages of Scripture related to sharing the heart of God with the world around us. In Matthew 5:13-16 Jesus taught:

You are the salt of the earth, but if salt has lost its taste, how shall its saltiness be restored? It is no longer good for anything except to be thrown out and trampled under people's feet. You are the light of the world. A city set on a hill cannot be hidden. Nor do people light a lamp and put it under a basket, but on a stand, and it gives light to all in the house. In the same way, let your light shine before others, so that they may see your good works and give glory to your Father who is in heaven.

One of the most powerful aspects of this passage is how Jesus begins by speaking identity over us. God doesn't tell us to go get some salt and share it. He says we are salt. He doesn't tell us to go get a light and shine it. He says we are a light. Sharing God's heart is a part of who we are. As believers we've been redeemed—washed clean—that we might proclaim the excellencies of our Savior by living in line with our new identity.

The world is a dark place. It is without hope. It's filled with the blind leading the blind and the needy seeking fulfillment from the needy. Our only hope is Jesus. The one, true Guide is the Holy Spirit.

We are called to a lifestyle of expelling the darkness around us with the powerful proclamation of God's heart to love, provide for, and redeem all those who would simply say yes to him. We are called to respond to Jesus' call and cease putting a basket over the light he's placed within us.

We don't have to be apologetic for the hope we have. We don't have to fear the opinion of man. We can love relentlessly, offer grace unexpectedly, and sacrifice ourselves so that others might see a glimpse of God's heart. *"Let your light shine before others"* today. Don't cover up who you are in Christ. Seek to reveal God's heart in all you do. And watch as the world around you is drawn to the light of God's unconditional love revealed through your life.

GUIDED PRAYER

1. Meditate on Jesus' words in the Sermon on the Mount. Renew your mind to who you are in Christ.

"You are the salt of the earth, but if salt has lost its taste, how shall its saltiness be restored? It is no longer good for anything except to be thrown out and trampled under people's feet. You are the light of the world. A city set on a hill cannot be hidden. Nor do people light a lamp and put it under a basket, but on a stand, and it gives light to all in the house. In the same way, let your light shine before others, so that they may see your good works and give glory to your Father who is in heaven." Matthew 5:13-16

2. In what ways are you covering up your light? In what ways are you living in fear or according to the ways of the world? Take time to engage in confession and receive God's forgiveness and love.

3. Receive courage from God to live in accordance with your new identity as salt and light. Ask God how you can be light in the darkness today. Ask him for specific ways you can reveal the hope you have in Jesus to others. Journal his response.

Oftentimes we see the things of God as a part of our life. As soon as God starts trying to change the way we live day-to-day, we put a wall up over our hearts so we don't have to change. But to sequester God is to value this life over eternity. To care more about the world's opinion of us than who God says we are is to try and make God a servant of the world and its systems. God is the Creator. He alone is King. And he alone knows best as our loving Father. To section off your life and allow God only into parts is to live foolishly. Crown God as King over every part of you. Choose to live as salt and light. And experience life where God is allowed to manifest himself, bless you in every way he can, and use your life to change the world for the better. May your day today be filled with all the fullness of God.

Extended Reading: Matthew 5

DEVOTIONAL

The idea of evangelism has always been terrifying to me. Going up to someone and interrupting their day to tell them about Jesus, no matter how real and good I know him to be, has never been comfortable for me. But you can't read Scripture and escape God's command to share the gospel. You can't read through the New Testament and discount the reality that the disciples gave themselves entirely—to the point of death—that the world might come to know Jesus.

"Go into all the world and proclaim the gospel to the whole creation."

MARK 16:15

Verses like Mark 16:15-16 couldn't be more clear. Jesus commands us, *"Go into all the world and proclaim the gospel to the whole creation. Whoever believes and is baptized will be saved, but whoever does not believe will be condemned."* Evangelism is meant to be a part of our normal lives. It's not just for the few. It's not just for pastors or the intensely extroverted. It's for you and me.

When I assess my own heart I discover that my fears related to evangelism are entirely selfish. In fact, I don't know if I could do something more selfish than hold back the one hope for the world just to protect my own image. Jesus is clear in Mark 16:16 that those who don't believe in him will be condemned. It's like I contain the cure for a deadly disease and rather than sacrificing my image to love them by sharing the one cure, I just let them continue to suffer.

In pondering my own heart I realize that the way to engage in evangelism isn't fixing myself; it's getting over myself. Is my image really so important that it's worth condemnation for another? Are the opinions of others really so important to me that I would withhold from them eternal, abundant life with a God who loves them relentlessly and perfectly?

I am made to share God's light. I have been commissioned by my King to go out and share his heart. It's time that we obey God's command in Philippians 2:3: *"Do nothing from selfish ambition or conceit, but in humility count others more significant than yourselves."* Sure, people might think I'm weird. Sure, it might be a little awkward. But God is after the hearts of his creation, and he's called me to help. May we be those who set aside our pride, seek humility, and love others whatever the cost. May we be so bold as to set our eyes on heaven and sacrifice this life for the sake of eternity. And may the world change around us as we humbly and courageously proclaim the goodness of our heavenly Father.

GUIDED PRAYER

1. Meditate on God's call for you to engage in evangelism.

"Go into all the world and proclaim the gospel to the whole creation. Whoever believes and is baptized will be saved, but whoever does not believe will be condemned."
Mark 16:15-16

"For the Son of Man came to seek and to save the lost."
Luke 19:10

"Therefore, we are ambassadors for Christ, God making his appeal through us. We implore you on behalf of Christ, be reconciled to God." 2 Corinthians 5:20

2. What are your fears in regard to evangelism?
What holds you back from telling others about the good news of God's unconditional love?

3. Take time to humble yourself before God and others. Ask him for grace to love others above yourself. Set your eyes on him and open your heart to receive his affection.

In Jesus' conclusion of the Great Commission he tells his disciples, *"And behold, I am with you always, to the end of the age"* (Matthew 28:20). Our power for evangelism is that God is with us. He doesn't send us out alone. His love, power, and presence are fully available to us when we seek to share the gospel with others. When you tell others about Jesus, don't speak of him as if he's not with you. Don't pray as if he doesn't move and work miracles. Instead, share the reality of God's nearness with a world that needs to be touched by a revelation of his love. May you be empowered to share the gospel with someone today that they might come to know the power and presence of God.

Extended Reading: Matthew 28

WEEK 4

DEVOTIONAL

One of the most impactful ways we can share God's heart with others is by living compassionately. To show compassion is to step outside of yourself and love another in times of weakness. And to live compassionately is to posture your heart continually toward giving grace and love to those who need it most.

"Be kind to one another, tenderhearted, forgiving one another, as God in Christ forgave you."

EPHESIANS 4:32

Very little stirs my heart to God more than compassion. When someone sees me in my imperfection and chooses to love me rather than cast me aside, my affection for them and God is automatically stirred. Oftentimes the world is too busy or self-focused to show compassion. We get too caught up in our plans, our needs, and our image to see the hurting and share God's heart.

But God is calling us to a life lived humbly and sacrificially. Philippians 2:4 says, *"Let each of you look not only to his own interests, but also to the interests of others."* The world is in desperate need of compassion. People need mercy and grace when they fail, show weakness, or are experiencing hard times. God's heart is to use us that we might show mercy and grace as a reflection of his unconditional love. He's calling us to be light in the darkness that the world might see in us the compassionate heart of our heavenly Father.

It's for this reason Paul writes in Ephesians 4:32, *"Be kind to one another, tenderhearted, forgiving one another, as God in Christ forgave you."* You can forgive because you've been forgiven. You can be kind because your Father has been nothing but kind to you. And you can be tenderhearted because God was so tender in heart toward you. He was so compassionate that he gave his life to free you, empower you, strengthen you, and ground you in his grace and love.

Take time in guided prayer to receive a fresh revelation of God's kindness, tenderness, and forgiveness. Open your heart and let him transform you to be more like him. Allow his heart to become your own. And live today in response to God's love by showing compassion to others that they might know the tenderness and mercy of your heavenly Father.

GUIDED PRAYER

1. Meditate on God's heart of kindness, tenderness, and forgiveness.

"But when the goodness and loving kindness of God our Savior appeared, he saved us, not because of works done by us in righteousness, but according to his own mercy, by the washing of regeneration and renewal of the Holy Spirit, whom he poured out on us richly through Jesus Christ our Savior." Titus 3:4-6

"And he arose and came to his father. But while he was still a long way off, his father saw him and felt compassion, and ran and embraced him and kissed him." Luke 15:20

"Out of the depths I cry to you, O Lord! O Lord, hear my voice! Let your ears be attentive to the voice of my pleas for mercy! If you, O Lord, should mark iniquities, O Lord, who could stand? But with you there is forgiveness, that you may be feared. I wait for the Lord, my soul waits, and in his word I hope." Psalm 130:1-5

2. Take a moment to receive the love of God. Open your heart to him and experience his kindness, tenderness, and forgiveness.

3. Ask God to empower you to show compassion today. Choose to live with your eyes not only set on your needs, but also on the needs of others.

"Finally, all of you, have unity of mind, sympathy, brotherly love, a tender heart, and a humble mind."
1 Peter 3:8

"Put on then, as God's chosen ones, holy and beloved, compassionate hearts, kindness, humility, meekness, and patience, bearing with one another and, if one has a complaint against another, forgiving each other; as the Lord has forgiven you, so you also must forgive."
Colossians 3:12-13

The only way we can live compassionately is by abiding in the love of our heavenly Father. 1 John 3:17 says, *"But if anyone has the world's goods and sees his brother in need, yet closes his heart against him, how does God's love abide in him?"* God's love transforms us. His heart empowers us to live differently. You can abide in the love of God today. You can live filled up with the knowledge of his grace and presence moment to moment and allow him to be your source. Don't live as if you serve a distant God. Live today in acknowledgement that he is closer to you than your breath—nearer to you than your own skin. The Holy Spirit dwells within you and longs to empower you with his love today. May you live compassionately today and see the lives of others impacted as you reflect the heart of your heavenly Father.

Extended Reading: Colossians 3

DEVOTIONAL

To live as an authentic disciple of Jesus is to live courageously. Jesus didn't call us to a life of shrinking back. We're not commanded to sit on the sidelines. He didn't call us to to pursue comfort, stability, approval with man, or societal status. He's called us to love unconditionally, give sacrificially, obey him unreservedly, and to live courageously. In John 15:19 Jesus clearly says, *"If you were of the world, the*

> *"Have I not commanded you? Be strong and courageous. Do not be frightened, and do not be dismayed, for the Lord your God is with you wherever you go."*
>
> **JOSHUA 1:9**

world would love you as its own; but because you are not of the world, but I chose you out of the world, therefore the world hates you." To be of God and practice the things of God is in powerful, direct opposition to the things of the world and its ruler, our enemy. For this reason God offers encouragement to those who face trial—to those who live courageously. 1 Peter 4:12-14 says:

Beloved, do not be surprised at the fiery trial when it comes upon you to test you, as though something strange were happening to you. But rejoice insofar as you share Christ's sufferings, that you may also rejoice and be glad when his glory is revealed. If you are insulted for the name of Christ, you are blessed, because the Spirit of glory and of God rests upon you.

God is calling you to a life far greater and more important than comfort and worldly pleasure. He's calling you to live by faith, believing that true blessing and true pleasure is found in him alone. He's calling you to step out of your former ways and live in accordance with his will that you might experience fullness of life in him.

For this reason Scripture says in Joshua 1:9, *"Have I not commanded you? Be strong and courageous. Do not be frightened, and do not be dismayed, for the Lord your God is with you wherever you go."* In the midst of any trial you can have transcendent, tangible comfort in God. In this midst of any suffering or pain you can find rest in the loving arms of your heavenly Father. And in the face of great opposition you can choose to live courageously. Your God is with you. He will never leave you. Courage comes from acknowledging the reality and power of God's nearness.

As we finish this week on sharing God's heart, find courage today to boldly love others. Take time to receive God's unconditional love and grace that you might share him with a world who desperately needs transcendent comfort and peace. Live courageously today and see heaven come to earth around you. Seek life and love in God alone. May your time of guided prayer be filled with encouragement from the Holy Spirit and the word of God.

GUIDED PRAYER

1. Meditate on the call of God to live courageously. Reflect on his promise to be with you always.

"Have I not commanded you? Be strong and courageous. Do not be frightened, and do not be dismayed, for the Lord your God is with you wherever you go." Joshua 1:9

"But we are not of those who shrink back and are destroyed, but of those who have faith and preserve their souls." Hebrews 10:39

"Even though I walk through the valley of the shadow of death, I will fear no evil, for you are with me; your rod and your staff, they comfort me." Psalm 23:4

2. Assess your own life. In what ways are you seeking worldly comfort over living courageously in God? What fears do you have about sharing God's heart that are winning out over courage from God?

"And as for what fell among the thorns, they are those who hear, but as they go on their way they are choked by the cares and riches and pleasures of life, and their fruit does not mature." Luke 8:14

3. Go to God with your fears and receive encouragement in him. Take time to rest in God's presence. Ask him for his perspective on that which hinders you from sharing his heart and living courageously. Journal his response.

"For God gave us a spirit not of fear but of power and love and self-control." 2 Timothy 1:7

When you choose to respond to God's call in faith, know that he will fill you with courage and boldness. The disciples were not naturally courageous people. Prior to the coming of the Holy Spirit they were weak, selfish, and cowardly. But in God they were made strong. In God they accomplished the impossible. In God they were used for eternal purposes that bore fruit you and I are still experiencing. Decide today to partner with God in seeing his kingdom come to earth through your life. Decide to jump in and be an active part of the spiritual awakening happening all around us. Decide to get off the sidelines of the Christian life and share God's heart with all those he leads you to. May your day be filled with boldness and courage in the Holy Spirit.

Extended Reading: Luke 8